The Unlearning Leader

The Unlearning Leader

Leading for Tomorrow's
Schools Today

Michael Lubelfeld and Nick Polyak

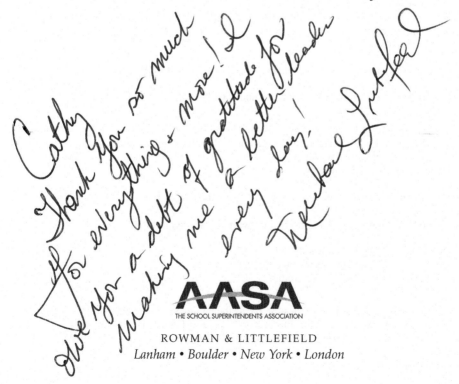

AASA
THE SCHOOL SUPERINTENDENTS ASSOCIATION

ROWMAN & LITTLEFIELD
Lanham • Boulder • New York • London

Published in partnership with the American Association of School Administrators

Published by Rowman & Littlefield
A wholly owned subsidiary of The Rowman & Littlefield Publishing Group, Inc.
4501 Forbes Boulevard, Suite 200, Lanham, Maryland 20706
www.rowman.com

Unit A, Whitacre Mews, 26-34 Stannary Street, London SE11 4AB

British Library Cataloguing in Publication Information Available

Library of Congress Cataloging-in-Publication Data Available

ISBN: 978-1-4758-3345-4 (cloth : alk. paper)
ISBN: 978-1-4758-3346-1 (pbk. : alk. paper)
ISBN: 978-1-4758-3347-8 (electronic)

™
♾ The paper used in this publication meets the minimum requirements of
American National Standard for Information Sciences—Permanence of Paper
for Printed Library Materials, ANSI/NISO Z39.48-1992.

Printed in the United States of America

Contents

Foreword

I smile at the stories told by many people my age about what technology and communication looked and sounded like when we were starting our careers. For gosh sakes, the new Nobel Prize winner for Literature, Bob Dylan, sang "The Times They Are a-Changin'" back in 1964. As Mike Lubelfeld and Nick Polyak so brilliantly capture in this book, the times are still changing, and so must we as leaders so that we may best serve our students.

In my desk drawer at home I still have a slide rule. Mike and Nick, have you ever used one of those? And I will confess to still having some 8-tracks that I can't bear to part with, and I have vinyl going back almost 100 years which we play on our Victrola with the crank on the side (a wonderful collector's item).

That change will happen is a certainty. Imagine what stories Mike and Nick will tell in years ahead about how they had to labor through lost cell tower signals when they drove out in the countryside, or how they be sure to charge their phones a couple of times a day to communicate.

Yet, the basic premise of this book is that, as constant as change is, the imperative for real change must be faced and addressed by all of us. As Mike and Nick share with us, "old conventions stymie meaningful change." While it may be cute and somewhat amusing to tell stories about what it used to be like "back in the day" when we were truly hard-wired to our computers, it's not so amusing to read or know of students who are not learning to the level they are capable of because the system has not unlearned limiting conventions.

I truly love Mike and Nick as my colleagues and teachers. They help me unlearn every time I talk to them. Yes, they also help me to learn. They are remarkable leaders having an impact on this generation of learners, not only in their home districts but with others who learn from them on Tweet chats,

Ignite Sessions, learning and studying together at professional consortia, and in teaching aspiring superintendents.

What they are asking of each of us is what other professions know well. Almost too obvious to state, doctors learn new procedures and treatments, professional baseball players unlearn bad habits at the plate so that they can learn new ones, pianists unlearn poor technique as they breathe joy into the notes on the page, and teachers move on from Warriner's *English Grammar and Composition* to Lucy Calkins's "Reading and Writing Project."

I did struggle with the problem that if we unlearn *everything*, there is the possibility of throwing out the baby with the bathwater. We don't have to unlearn everything, do we? Certainly, there are evidence-based, forward-learning practices, beliefs, and visionary statements which serve us well. In working through that question, I came to more fully appreciate and respect the compelling unlearning arguments of Mike and Nick.

Of course, we stand on the shoulders of many wonderful learners from many generations. However, each generation took the issues of their day and moved ahead in a meaningful way. For example, communication is not a new issue for educators. It's how we look at the essential question of how to best communicate with our students, our staff, our colleagues, and our communities that we gain insight if we "stop, think, act" with a whole new set of opportunities.

As I struggle to put down my pencil and pad for gathering my thoughts, tomorrow's leaders will struggle to move on from blogging, tweeting, and messaging. We must, as learners and leaders, be deliberate and aware of our need to continually unlearn and learn anew. This is a cognitive process not left to chance.

The authors write that their "aim is to share, collaborate, communicate, create, and think critically in support of growth, learning, and success." Mike and Nick, thank you for making us think and unlearn as we learn together.

Morton Sherman, EdD, associate executive director,
American Association for School Administrators (AASA)

Preface

The Time is Now

In some school systems, the executive leadership still does not understand or value current methods of communication, especially technological methods. Their relative lack of knowledge about social connectivity can become quite detrimental to a school system in search of change, innovation, and leadership. We want to help school leaders unlearn their current approaches to leadership in how they "connect," lead, support student learning, transform schools, and impact organizational culture.

We wrote this book to celebrate the connected leader, show case study examples of change and modern change processes, and to help leaders unlearn to relearn! The premise of this book is that we all need to unlearn. Our landscape is applied to leadership, classrooms, pedagogy, and education in general. In order to change and prepare for tomorrow, we submit that much of what we have learned must be unlearned as we aim to create a new tomorrow for our nation's children.

Our current public school system was essentially created by ten university leaders in the 1890s. A lot has changed since then, yet our structures in public schools seem unable to unlearn the structures and conventions from the nineteenth century. Our purposes include supporting leaders to lead and enabling leaders to lead for tomorrow's schools. There is an urgency for change.

Futurist Jack Uldrich has made presentations across the country about the concept of unlearning. While at a Future Ready Summit in Illinois, we participated in an activity that has been practiced across the country from Jack and others. We were asked one simple question, "What color are yield signs?" Sounds simple. Uldrich asked the audience to raise their hands if they thought yield signs are yellow and black.

The majority of those in the audience raised their hands in a sign of agreement that yield signs are yellow and black. That was the correct answer, many years ago when members in the audience first learned about yield signs. Years after the audience members learned the yellow and black color scheme the yield signs across the country changed to red and white.

Folks knew intellectually that the signs were no longer yellow and black, but they "learned" this earlier in their lives and knowledge proves difficult to unlearn. This provides a powerful lesson about our need to unlearn old knowledge in order to modernize our thinking as to what is true today. And it shows the challenge. That which leaders learned early on in their careers, or in leadership schools, often stifles their growth with their inability to unlearn.

The world is changing at an exponential pace, but often times our educational leaders and our educational systems are not. This experience (with the yield sign) was an epiphany of sorts for both of us that has led us to look at educational leadership through the lens of unlearning (retrieved from https:// www.youtube.com/watch?v=N7MfbCWHRto).

Horace Mann is credited with saying "Education then, beyond all other devices of human origin, is the great equalizer of the conditions of men, the balance-wheel of the social machinery." Now, more than ever, leaders need to unlearn and they need to unleash powerful innovation in the new reality. Today is far different from yesterday. Leaders must get out from behind their desks and integrate doing and empowering others with managing and leading from a 30,000 foot view.

Since 1983 our nation's schools have been at risk. Since 2002 we have been leaving no child behind. Now with ESEA reauthorization, we are getting ready for every student to succeed. In order for every student to succeed, school leaders must unlearn the old ways and learn and practice leadership through innovative methods and courageous actions.

Representing careers in leadership and public education spanning many decades and impacting thousands of K–12 students and teachers, we are sharing a passion for excellence in education with the leadership lessons and insights throughout this book. We serve as educational leaders as part of a larger calling to serve. We wrote this book as part of this calling.

Students in each grade level have but one chance to experience that grade level. Students don't have time to wait. We mentioned a sense of urgency—the urgency is that the nineteenth-century structures no longer serve as relevant to the needs of modern society. Why has it been so hard to change structures in schools? We submit that it is part of the challenge of unlearning. "Everyone" has attended school—they have a construct as to what it should be.

We are learned leaders in the education space. We too were schooled in traditional, nineteenth-century structures though we have enjoyed success and fulfilment. And we are from another era than our students. It's incumbent upon us as leaders to demonstrate an organizational agility and flexibility so that the current needs of children are reflected in the nation's schools. We have a moral imperative, an economic imperative, a pedagogical imperative, and a leadership imperative to unlearn.

Just because our teachers, leaders, members of elected boards of education, parents, grandparents, and community at large learned what school is—in another era—that does not mean we current leaders need to lead for nostalgia. Nostalgia has a place—in museums and other venues, but not in schools. Unlearning individuals' experiences proves quite difficult. Learning is wired and challenging to unlearn.

Policymakers don't know what is current in education—they know what made them successful and happy—they don't know what is needed now since often they are many levels removed from schooling. Yet it is policymakers who are credited with legislating mandates, standards, expectations, training, rules, etc., yet they base their views on their own construct of education and schooling—that of nostalgia.

We wrote this book because nostalgic policies might be destroying public education. Nostalgic experiences are actually incongruous with the information generation. Voices in telephone devices can restate the 50 state capitals—that doesn't mean it's not important to learn the 50 state capitals, it means that memorization is not the only form of "learning" anymore. Just because you, your parents, your grandparents and your great-grandparents also memorized capitals in fourth grade does not mean that it's relevant for today's youth.

We wrote this book because leaders who unlearn and innovate make possible opportunities for children. We wrote this book because leaders can unlearn ways of the past to create new and relevant futures. We wrote this book because so many great coaches and mentors and friends guide and support our unlearning and we feel called to share and illustrate how unlearning is impacting systems in our care. The time is now to change, unlearn, create a new system and a new constructs for schooling—we have the knowledge and we have the will, let's unlearn together!

Acknowledgments

For many years, we have been fortunate to have mentors and guides who have helped our careers and our professional learning. We are indebted to the great resources and help of the Illinois Association of School Administrators (IASA), and the American Association of School Administrators (AASA). In addition, we have learned more than anticipated from the Twitter PLN we are lucky to interact with.

We are grateful for the support, guidance, and mentorship of so many leaders, coaches, and friends in terms of our leadership journeys and our own unlearning. From organizational leadership at the AASA like Dan Domenech and Mort Sherman, at the IASA like Brent Clark and Rich Voltz, our spouses Kate, Stephanie, our collective children (Chase, Maya, John, Justin, Ben, and Gabe), our co-workers, our friends who contributed to this book, and many others—so many support our work and influence our leadership allowing us to learn, unlearn, and grow every day!

To our collective Boards of Education and to each member with whom we have served, we thank you for supporting our vision, our leadership styles, our personal professional growth and learning, for giving us the chance to serve our communities, and for putting up with us.

—Nick Polyak and Michael Lubelfeld

To Jim Newlin—I have finished the first set of homework ... I'm always grateful to you, my friend, for seeing around corners I could not see—I'm always seeking new assignments!

—Michael Lubelfeld

List of Tables and Figures

TABLES

FIGURES

Introduction

School leadership positions can still be considered to be lonely and isolating. *The Unlearning Leader: Leading for Tomorrow's Schools Today* contains lessons and action steps that will change the reality of school leaders from lone wolves to pack leaders. Through modern technological tools like Twitter, barriers are broken down and walls become windows and doors as leaders from all over the world connect and share leadership lessons.

Our aim is to share through recent experience, impactful readings, professional reflections, and replicable suggestions, how educators can open the doors for connected culture building and connected educating in their organizations and lives to lead tomorrow's schools. Our aim is to show how nineteenth-century structures are no longer relevant and it's proving quite difficult for the system to unlearn, however, WE can unlearn through deliberate actions.

The leadership framework upon which our work as leaders has been built relates to the writings of Kouzes and Posner (2012). In their book *The Leadership Challenge—Five Exemplary Practices of Leadership: Model the Way, Inspire a Shared Vision, Challenge the Process, Enable Others to Act and Encourage the Heart (MICEE)* they support through research how these exemplary leadership practices do, in fact, impact leaders and organizations.

In each of the first five chapters we share a mid-chapter sidebar feature highlighting and focusing on each of the five exemplary practices of leadership. It is important for leaders to unlearn their old practices and to relearn and reimagine how MICEE principles and practices will guide us for tomorrow's schools. Through practice we show how research, studies, evidence, and literature about leadership can be implemented.

The learning purposes of this book include:

- Energize people to think, act, and do leadership differently
- Embody an innovative mindset at all levels that supports unlearning
- Model and share through experience, observation, and trial and error a new way of leading from within the organization
- Put forth the power and positive impact and legacy for leadership
- Unlearn old truths to begin to lead in new ways
- Leverage connection opportunities like #suptchat to lead and learn for tomorrow

The Unlearning Leader: Leading for Tomorrow's Schools Today shares actionable steps and suggestions for how to build and impact organizational culture, support connectivity, and focus on student learning and staff growth. This is a book that allows for replication of ideas, behaviors, and initiatives to help districts move forward to meet the needs of tomorrow's students. Through case studies and real examples of systems change, ideas and methods are shared and illustrated.

From our own experiences as leaders as well as from our learnings from the literature, we share, we communicate, and we encourage the reader to unlearn and create new realities. The learning purposes of this book are woven throughout each section, each chapter, each vignette, and each page.

We have been superintendents, executive administrators, and teachers for more than forty years combined in six different school systems spanning grades PK–12 in suburban, rural, and urban settings. While traditional schooling and the nineteenth-century structures inherent in traditional schooling structures have been successful for many, including us, we realize through our work and life that the world is now different. Even though we have been successful as a result of old conventions, we know and lead for new conventions.

In order to compete as a nation, catch up and succeed as a society, educational leaders need to unlearn the foundational structures of the nineteenth century and reimagine schooling. We have a passion for education and a calling to leadership and service. Through our leadership work and experiences leading organizations, we have unlearned, relearned, and grown in support of tomorrow's schools.

The premise of this book is that a leader's vision and leadership combined with specific actions will increase efficacy, engagement, inspiration, empowerment, and ultimately student learning and student success. We believe that leaders must unlearn many concepts and experiences that have served them well if we are to create a new reality for today's and tomorrow's students.

A main purpose of this book is to highlight how the modern leader thrives in the connected world and how ubiquitous technological tools remove the once lonely nature of leadership positions like the superintendency, the principalship, or the classroom teacher. In addition, in order to lead, future leaders need to unlearn what worked as they grew up in their world.

The idea of unlearning the traditional A–F letter grade systems which made many of us successful in favor of standards-based grading is a reality that exists today in many K–12 and higher education systems. Unlearning nineteenth-century ingrained practices, like rows of desks, batch processing, top down structures, and more is being preached by educational thought leaders such as Sir Ken Robinson and others.

This practical book is needed since the literature is often missing the voice of the modern practicing school leaders who unlearn the past tactics deliberately, intentionally, and collaboratively in support of adult, community, and student growth and learning for the future. This book is a practitioners' guide and is also written for university leadership preparation programs, for lawmakers paving the way for innovation, and for leadership support to help put theory into practice.

This book is intended for superintendents, central office and school administrators, School Board members, school leaders, classroom teachers, parents, business people, policymakers, educational leadership professors and adjunct faculty, and graduate students in educational leadership programs. Anyone interested in change, growth, leadership, and social media tools as communication levers will benefit from the lessons we share on the pages that follow.

In chapter 1, we address "connection" and the change process. How do leaders connect and network today versus the past? We confront long-held beliefs that the superintendent position is lonely, for example, and challenge the process for networking and for leading systems change.

In chapter 2, "Unlearning Planning and Change Process," the Reflection Questions are:

Do you think that leaders should wait and observe for a year before making changes? Have you successfully implemented change? How do you measure effectiveness?

In chapter 3, we share another set of examples about how leaders can unlearn the concept of "waiting" to implement change through a case study like set of examples from a three-year-change process.

In chapter 4, the topics we have addressed in #suptchat are varied and reflect the multitude of complex challenges leaders face every day in all settings across the country (and world).

In chapter 5, we discuss the need to think differently about how we learn in schools and unlearn old practices of professional learning at the micro and macro levels. In addition, we share personal professional stories about the impact of professional association partnerships on their practice.

In chapter 6, the overall topic of leadership is addressed from the unlearning perspectives. Topics in this chapter address flexibility, visibility, compassion, and service. Each chapter has an end-of-chapter commentary from a leader in leadership.

This book explores effective leadership techniques and results that can be replicated to change public education in the United States. We present a vision and a reality that leaders, teachers, board members, and policymakers can apply to their current situations.

The Unlearning Leader: Leading for Tomorrow's Schools Today includes a series of unique elements, including: (a) reflective questions that unpack the essential queries for each chapter with a stop-think-act feature; (b) a unique end-of-chapter feature, SUPTCHAT: Stop, Understand, Plan, Think, where suggested actions and reflected questions are tied to the letters from the monthly superintendent Twitter chat which exemplifies new leading and learning; and (c) a relationship between new learning and leading methods related to evidence-based practices from Kouzes and Posner.

Finally, each chapter will include a practitioner commentary from successful educational leaders across the country. Each additional voice comes from our colleagues and friends we have met through a variety of programs in the Illinois Association of School Administrators (IASA), the Suburban School Superintendents (SSS), and the American Association of School Administrators (AASA). We know you will enjoy the change of voice and the superior wisdom that our friends provide.

Chapter One

Unlearning Connections

You can't fall if you don't climb. But there's no joy in living your whole life on the ground.

—Unknown

Reflection Questions

In what ways do you consider yourself a connected educator?
Have you called a neighboring educator this week?
Do you regularly assess your ability to listen? How can you do this?

Stop-Think-Act

Can you identify communication methods your organization uses that are effective?
Do you know why Twitter chats are so popular with educators?
They say our profession is lonely. Intentionally take steps to be connected, break the cycle of loneliness—reach out.

PAST COMMUNICATIONS

In the old days classroom teachers closed their doors and worked individually. School leaders generally kept to themselves or their local region. The main sources of "new" information were likely written months or years earlier.

Times have changed. Ten years ago, superintendents and principals used the U.S. Postal Service to support communication and leadership. They used paper memos and inter-office envelopes and even *voicemail*. Teachers would send a paper newsletter home each week. Communication today is instant and immediate. Today's superintendents, today's teachers, and today's students are connected 24/7 and are able to communicate with blogs, audio, video, text messaging, e-mail, and any number of social media applications like Twitter, Facebook, Instagram, Remind, Voxer, Snapchat, etc.

The past ten years have shown significant changes in terms of consumption of information and "fingertip" access. Yes, times have changed. Communication has changed, but the *importance* of communication in support of leadership and innovation remains the same. Today's superintendent knows how to leverage the power of technology to harness effective and impactful communication. Today's teachers share learning examples in real time.

When Nick first came to Leyden in 2013, he left behind a fairly traditional system and arrived at Leyden Community High District which had undergone a transition to Google Apps for Education. In the first week on the job, he sent an e-mail to the administrative team and attached a Microsoft Word document. One of the other school leaders replied to the e-mail with one word, "Seriously?"

Leyden had already unlearned old practices for sharing information and had moved on to the collaborative use of Google Docs to share and work together. Nick was forced to unlearn the practice of making changes to a document, renaming it, and sending it to the next person for edits. He had to admit that he needed to modernize his practices to meet the needs of his team and his school district.

During in-services and meetings in recent years, school leaders have shared videos on YouTube in the "Did You Know" series (https://www.youtube.com/watch?v=YmwwrGV_aiE) where they show statistics about the number of e-mails sent, the users of Facebook, technology impacts of the modern world, etc. The messages from these videos also support, explain, and define this generation's ubiquitous relationship with technology. These videos are also out of date by the time anyone views them.

As we write in 2016, it is difficult to imagine that it has only been six years since people first began using iPads. Now it is impossible to go anywhere and not see people using iPads. How has our world changed so much that a device no one knew about six years ago, introduced five years ago, is now in the hands of more than 200 million people globally?

The iPad is a perfect representation of our culture's demand for constant connectivity. Yet, despite these profound and deeply rooted changes in society, as mentioned in the preface of this book, in some school systems the top leadership still does not understand or value current methods of communication. Their relative lack of knowledge about social connectivity can become detrimental to a school system in search of change, innovation, and leadership.

Students today will be competing for jobs that do not yet exist. Students today will be connecting in ways that generations of educators do not yet understand. It is incumbent upon all educators to connect, to open up, to model, and to essentially lead in a culture of connected communication. In order for innovative teachers to be supported in their growth, it is incumbent upon top leaders to demonstrate support for innovation and risk taking. It's time for many to unlearn.

CONNECTED EDUCATOR

The "connected educator" is a hot topic today. These are the educators and educational leaders who are learning and growing through multiple digital learning networks. These personal and professional learning networks allow people at various levels to share links, blogs, journals, research, advice, tips, tricks, etc. Connections must be made at home and out of the region, in person and virtually.

These social and online professional networks like Twitter allow for virtual relationships to develop between and among professionals at many levels. These networks are the wave of the present and future—not the past. These networks are revolutionizing professional development and conferences. Now terms like "un conference" or "ed camp" are becoming the norm. Now internal "experts"—meaning professionals at every level—are facilitating sessions and sharing creativity with one another.

Casas et al. (2015) write about why it matters to get connected (xix). They write that connected educators do different "things" in terms of leadership. Their definition of connected educators is "ones who are actively and constantly seeking new opportunities and resources to grow as professionals" (xxiii). From their work, our work and experiences, and the values we place on being connected, we are sharing a brief list of what makes an educator connected.

- Organizing the entire community around specific and focused goal areas.
- Building relationships online and in person.
- Seeking feedback, sharing feedback, and incorporating feedback into actions.
- Staying focused on the big picture, medium picture, and the details.
- Reaching beyond the "walls" of the district and community to learn, grow, and share.
- Responding to inquiries (press, parents, students, community members, and stakeholders) in a timely and respectful manner.
- Using technology as an accelerator for teaching, learning, and leading.
- Measuring culture and deliberately working to improve organizational culture.
- Keeping students, staff, and community at the forefront of all decision-making.

The superintendent who is connected with stakeholders demonstrates how to meet the needs of the adult learners so that they may be supported in meeting the needs of the children. For schools to change—for school systems to change—for instruction to change—so must our leadership lenses. Unlearning as a concept calls for review, reimagining, and replacement of current paradigms.

Connected leaders and teachers are deliberate and intentional about turning learning opportunities into connections and networks; the leader is demonstrating leading by example and connecting. When a leader is asking teachers what their needs are, following up with learning opportunities reflective of those needs, and communicating through words and actions (i.e., attending conferences arm-in-arm) they are connecting and leading through that experience.

SHARING AND CONNECTING: TWITTER AS A TOOL FOR GROWING CAPACITY

Twitter is perhaps the most powerful and meaningful social communication tool in the market today. It provides networking, learning and growth, and supports the value of communication and collaboration. This free tool connects leaders and learners instantly with text, imagery, and video.

Best of all, Twitter chats offer free professional learning in a venue where status and title are of little importance compared to the value of a great idea. The unlearning leader realizes that titles have a place—a very limited place—yet being open to ideas and concepts from all people at all levels is proving far more impactful than restricting connections based on referent titles.

Social media tools have allowed leaders to solve a real challenge and opportunity in the school districts where we have served and currently serve. In general, teachers are provided with a limited amount of planning time coupled with some professional collaboration time, but most of that time ends up being used as adult-focused learning time. Discussion about teaching and learning, and planning for teaching and learning, take place in earnest. Links to practical and applicable tools and resources are instant via Twitter and other social media platforms.

Twitter was opened and unblocked in both of our school districts because of the power of this social media tool. Used effectively, Twitter can help solve the problem of disconnection. Often tangible examples of new learning and new connections don't take place in typical/traditional meetings. Leaders who only engage in traditional meeting formats do not know what they are missing. And they are missing a lot.

We are amazed at the amount of incredible bloggers, tweeters, and leaders we have "interacted" with online and in person. Check out those we follow on Twitter (@npolyak and @mikelubelfeld) for the amazing leaders who are sharing information, collaborating and demonstrating, and illustrating leadership across state lines and international boundaries.

Through the use of our districts' hashtags #leydenpride and #engage109, teachers are now able to show what learning looks like and what innovation means in real life and in real time. More importantly, students are able to share those same things and take ownership of the districts' stories. Parents and community stakeholders can see, live, what learning looks like.

Social media has allowed for "wall dropping"—the walls between us no longer inhibit connections! Social media is taking connectivity to levels never before imagined. Using social media intentionally and deliberately caused us to unlearn a fear that is prevalent in many school systems. Fear of the "what if …" can cripple innovation, change, transformation, and growth. This is why leaders must unlearn a fear of the unknown in order to grow and prepare for tomorrow's schools. Leading for tomorrow's schools demands unlearning today.

Nick often tells stories about how he is able to use Twitter to connect with individuals in his schools and in his community. In his first year at Leyden, he cancelled school one day after a snowstorm. He took a picture of a cement bench, shown in figure 1.1, at one of the high schools and sent out a tweet telling everyone to stay warm on their day off.

By including #leydenpride in the tweet, the entire Leyden community was able to see that post, including the School Board President, Greg Ignoffo.

Figure 1.1   Leyden Bench.

Minutes later, Greg replied to Nick's tweet and said, "You know, the prior superintendent never used to call snow days." The power of that exchange lies in what it says about relationships and about the culture at Leyden.

That anecdote shows that the superintendent and the board president have a very positive relationship and it does that in a way that is transparent and public to the whole community. In many places, a superintendent or a board president are people that are often unseen, but social media allows us all to meet on the same platform.

When leaders take the time to connect and share on social media, those types of exchanges can happen on any level. When students tweet to #leydenpride to share about their college acceptances letters, their fine arts performances, or their athletic contests, Nick is able to reply and congratulate or encourage them.

He is able to meet students where they are and make personal connections with them. It may seem like a minor thing, but Nick revels in the moments where a student stops him in the hallway and says, "Are you Dr. Polyak? You liked my tweet!"

Unlearn some of the reasons people don't use social media. Through our collective support for and use of social media we have had multiple conversations with leaders and teachers about why they don't, or others should not use social media. "It's too public," "What if there are negative comments?," "What about screen time?" are just a few common criticisms.

Well, social media is public—everything posted is permanent. There likely will be negative comments. In our shared experiences the positive outweighs the negative by a wide margin. Screen time is relevant, and it's up to the family to determine how much screen time their child will have at home. In school, we support a balanced approach.

Twitter allows for cross-country collaboration as well. For example, Dr. Shane Hotchkiss, a superintendent colleague of ours in Pennsylvania sent us a Tweet and asked if we knew of a first grade teacher willing to connect with a first grade teacher in his district. So Mike sent out a Tweet using #engage109 and, lo and behold, he found a match!

It is amazing that, through Twitter, school leaders in different states are able to connect in new and different ways. The teachers and their first grade students collaborated in ways only possible and permissible with new, current, and modern tools. They used a class blog to teach each other about their communities. This writing for an authentic audience, in grade 1, had a whole new world opened and it started with a Tweet.

In addition, the teachers and students used other technological applications to create visuals of both communities. "The kids created pic collages with pictures around Deerfield. We also learned via Twitter about our weather differences between locations," shared Deerfield first grade teacher Kellie Cacioppo.

Through actions and deliberate methods, we are creating a culture of connectivity! It's no surprise that in 2016 Kellie wrote and earned an innovation grant introducing her first grade students to robotics and coding. Leadership that supports new approaches and unlearns the old industrial paradigm prepares superstars like Kellie and others for limitless growth and opportunity.

Twitter is quite possibly the best source of professional learning for educators and educational leaders; it's free, it breaks barriers of time and space, and it's full of thought leaders who show innovation and leadership in real time and in real settings. School leaders are finding more and more connections with like-minded and unlike-minded people who affirm that which works and who challenge that which can work better!

As Twitter fans and supporters, it is empowering to learn from so many around the country and world on a regular basis. Twitter chats, like #suptchat for superintendents, allow idea sharing, professional learning, and overall growth and support for educators at all levels. We will devote much of chapter 4 to the #suptchat leadership lessons.

The main goal for superintendents and all school leaders, educators, teachers, school service personnel, etc. is student learning and growth. The eyes on the prize as shared before are on student support, student learning, community engagement, teacher training and development, and learning!

Finally, applying effective instruction for students and staff connects the leader with the needs of the organization. Whether it is through Twitter, Facebook, Instagram, Voxer, blogging, Remind, e-mail, video messaging, text messaging, or whatever tools emerge next, communication best practices demand our attention as leaders so that we can tell our stories, engage our communities, inspire our students and staff, and empower each other to learn and grow each day.

MODEL THE WAY (SIDEBAR—MID-CHAPTER FEATURE)

The first of the five exemplary practices of leadership described and discerned from Kouzes and Posner's legendary book *The Leadership Challenge* is *Model the Way*. The authors of the Leadership Challenge explain that managers or leaders who are admired (across industry) share the following traits: honesty, forward thinking, competent, and inspiring.

> Statistical analyses revealed that a leader's behavior explains the vast majority of constituents' workplace engagement. A leader's actions contribute more to such factors as commitment, loyalty, motivation, pride, and productivity than does any other single variable. (p. 25)

Part of modeling the way requires that a leader knows her/his core values. Admired leaders can identify and name their core values, then they lead according to those values. When leading workshops, We take participants through a values exercise. In this exercise, the participant is given nearly 100 "value cards" (cards with common values like honesty, integrity, achievement, family, etc.).

Participants also have several categories in which they can place the value cards from seldom valued to always valued. It is a difficult process, but they need to identify their top 3–5 values. Their challenge is to discover if their self-perception of their core values matches the perception that others have of them? In order to model the way, the leader must first know what they really stand for—then they can model the way while staying true to their core values.

We try to model the way through our own connected style. We work with and learn from leaders in our own systems and those from all over our state, the nation, and the world. We attempt to model listening, learning, and acting.

We are proud of the results found in our systems thanks to our amazing teams. We try to model the way by sharing powerful learning and leading lessons like the value card activity.

We learned about many fundamental leadership activities and exercises while part of formal programs that will be described in greater detail in chapter 5. We try to walk the walk and talk the talk through seeking input, sharing input, and acting on the input. We try to demonstrate the exemplary practice of modeling the way in many ways on a regular basis.

By actively using social media to learn, share, and connect, we are showing others that we value this mode of connection. By hosting a Twitter chat, that will be described in greater detail in chapter 4, we are modeling professional connection, sacrifice, openness, and an insatiable desire to learn and lead. We also model unlearning by doing things differently and pivoting, or changing mid-stream, when circumstances dictate flexibility.

LISTENING

Each and every new leadership position starts with a transition period. The transition period, often called "the first 90 days" relates to connecting. In this chapter, in an effort to set the stage for leading and before we comment on technology age communication in the next section, we will emphasize the skill and act of listening.

A symbol that Mike has framed in his office is the Mandarin Chinese symbol for listening: the heart, ears, eyes ... together—Listen (shown in figure 1.2). In addition, both of us have participated in advanced leadership programs at the state and national levels. One of the cornerstones of those programs was effective leadership through listening.

Learning to truly listen is a skill that connects leaders. A listening framework with which we have become familiar comes from Theory U (Scharmer). The unlearning leader often has to unlearn how they listen so that they can create conditions of trust and empathy through changed actions.

Other examples of listening are on the macro, or organizational level. For example, using survey data, clearly and widely sharing the data in a feedback loop, and then acting on the input is an observable example of listening. It's incumbent on the leader to show the people what stakeholders said and reported in the survey, and to identify how that feedback was used to design the subsequent learning opportunities.

When we first became superintendents, and when we took our second superintendent posts, in our first 90 days, we called key stakeholders (clergy, government officials, parent organization leaders, financial officials, other educators in the area, etc.) and held personal meetings with as many people as

Figure 1.2   Chinese Character for Listening.

we could. If you have not already done so, seek out "focus groups" of people and ask them to talk to you.

Listening is a powerful communication tool and it supports culture building. Organizations can unlearn the idea that referent authority is the answer—it's actually referent authority impacted by listening and working with all members of the organization that is the answer. The incorporation of technology is an accelerator. It accelerates information transmission, communication, and used effectively, it improves listening.

TECHNOLOGY AGE COMMUNICATION

When leaders listen to the voice of the people and connect with them, they are acknowledging their importance. When they are deliberate and intentional about turning learning opportunities into connections and networks, school leaders are demonstrating leading by example and connecting. Technology offers many ways to get questions out to large numbers of people so that feedback can be shared in short periods of time.

Table 1.1   Listening Levels

Downloading	When you operate from Level 1 Listening	The conversation reconfirms what you already knew. You reconfirm your habits of thought: "There (s)he goes again!"
Factual Listening	When you operate from Level 2 Listening	You disconfirm what you already know and notice what is new out there: "This looks so different today!"
Empathic Listening	When you choose to operate from Listening 3	Your perspective is redirected to seeing the situation through the eyes of another: "Yes, now I really understand how you feel about it. I can sense it now too."
Generative Listening	And finally, when you choose to operate from Listening 4	You realize that by the end of the conversation you are no longer the same person you were when it began. You have gone through a subtle but profound change that has connected you to a deeper source of knowing, including the knowledge of your best future possibility and self.

Source: Content from Scharmer, Otto. (2007). *Theory U: Leading from the Future as It Emerges.* Cambridge, MA: Society for Organizational Learning.

When a leader asks teachers what their needs are or a teacher asks students the same, following up with learning opportunities reflective of those needs communicates a partnership in education. Technology tools allow for sorting, categorizing, establishing trends of data, and making meaning out of input. Taking input and acting on the input—and telling the stakeholders what you did with the input—can be done with relative ease using technological tools.

Technology age communication is all about connecting with others, leading others, and leveraging the tools of the trade to do so. As research about student learning shows, students learn and grow more when they have "choice and voice" in their learning. "Getting students into the game means creating a classroom climate that allows them to take risks and make mistakes" (Nash, 2016, p. 12). None of this is possible if leaders don't make the time to listen.

Adult learners also learn and grow more when they also have a voice in their learning and development. Unlearning the need to be "perfect" goes a long way to creating multiple learning labs and multiple opportunities to fail forward. When employees feel respected and valued they have a greater likelihood of following through with the initiatives. Technology tools allow for the leader to engage with more people in shorter periods of time.

A leader's direct connection with staff, aside from classroom visits is through professional learning. By sitting side by side for part or all of workshops and conferences, the school leader is demonstrating that he/she values the work of the teachers.

One leadership suggestion is to treat most days like the first 90—effective leaders actually never stop connecting and reaching out—and in doing so they open their minds to new ideas, affirm those ideas they know are correct, and work to impact change, and growth and transformation for the thousands of students whose education is, in part, under their control.

Whether you have one school, five schools, or 300 schools, you can connect by reaching out and asking people to speak with you—it's amazing how much people value time with school leaders. Once you start these relationships, all that follows—adult learning, student engagement, problem solving, community growth—work better, smoother, and in a more fulfilling connected way. Repeat your first 90 days from time to time! Relationships are an underpinning foundation for growth and professional development as well.

One way to turn this disconnected experience into an experience designed to breed connectivity can be found by intentionally aiming to form a lasting relationship. The leader who deliberately seeks out connections and opportunities to network, share, learn, and grow is the one who is leading that way on the home turf too.

SUMMARY

Times have changed. Ten years ago people relied on the U.S. Postal Service to support communication and leadership. They used paper memos and inter-office envelopes. Even though the past ten years have shown significant changes in terms of consumption of information and "fingertip" access, the *importance* of communication in support of leadership and innovation remains the same.

The unlearning is the "how" to communicate, the "why" is still the same as communication remains a foundation of trusting relationships. In chapter 2, you will learn how the over analysis of planning led to stymied change. Too often analysis has led to paralysis in school reform efforts. We show how *doing* change transforms an organization.

We share concrete examples from our respective school systems as examples of how our unlearning has led and continues to lead to second order changes on behalf of students, staff, and community. In chapter 2, the focus is on unlearning the change process and leading change powerfully and meaningfully in new and different ways. The use of technology, the leveraging of connectivity, and the unlearning of old long-held beliefs are essential to take organizations to higher levels.

S—Stop and reflect on the main ideas of this chapter. How could you implement one or more of the suggestions: seek input from stakeholders—share the data—take action as a result? If not, what steps can you take to be a better listener in your schools and your community?

U—Understand the need for connection inside and outside of your organization. Through what methods and strategies are you acting on communication needs in your organization?

P—Plan for how next week you will start the process of connecting with stakeholders using technological tools. Plan a meeting with your union or faculty leadership and engage in two-way conversations about communication in your district. Take input and plan with them.

T—Think of a key take-away from this chapter you will present at your next leadership team meeting; write it down.

Chat: Pick an edchat, like #suptchat or a state edchat and participate for an hour—if you do this regularly, make a point to respond to questions; if you have not yet done this, now is the time to experience a digital form of professional development. The concept of #suptchat will be expanded upon in chapter 4. This URL contains a listing of many education-related Twitter chats: https://sites.google.com/site/twittereducationchats/education-chat-calendar.

PRACTITIONER COMMENTARY—BRIAN TROOP

Dr. Brian Troop is the superintendent of the 4,200 student Ephrata Area School District in Ephrata, Pennsylvania.

A Network of Trusted Peers

I believe that the current reality of tightening budgets, increased legislative requirements, and instantaneous access to enormous quantities of information on "best-practice" strategies all combine to make the modern day district superintendent role more demanding and complex than it has ever been. Like any top-of-the-organizational-chart position, the superintendency is often a lonely job that offers minimal opportunity for true collaboration in facing this increasing complexity.

This perfect storm of factors makes establishing membership in a network of trusted peers one of the most valued assets for any superintendent. To perform at a high level a modern day superintendent needs to be *connected*. Connected not only to a local network of fellow superintendents, but to a broader network of trusted peers whose scope is well beyond the local level.

The ability to leverage technology and social media tools available today to establish and maintain professional relationships with like-minded superintendents from across the country is one of the most valuable skills for any educational leader. The value of the resources and expertise available to a connected school leader through his/her network of trusted colleagues is immeasurable.

To establish a trusting relationship with others in the same position, requires the establishment of a relationship through ongoing communication. Two decades ago, this was accomplished by superintendents in most areas of the country by scheduling regular golf games and long lunch meetings with colleagues who were geographically located in such a way where this was practical. This certainly limited the scope of diversity, expertise, and experience one could have in a network, not to mention the challenges of both time and perception that would be associated with a "regular golf game" appearing on any public official's schedule.

While reaching beyond that network of trusted colleagues was possible 20 years ago via telephone, U.S. Mail, or e-mail, it was the exception and only offered an acquaintance level of relationship. The lower level of trust associated with these types of communications did not provide the same benefits as interactions with trusted peers.

The local network is certainly still a valued asset in dealing with the common challenges and political nature of public school leadership. Collaboration on specific district initiatives and the growing reality of districts needing to achieve the efficiencies of shared service contracts at the local level are two huge factors that demonstrate the value of collaboration across district boundaries with those serving students in similar geographic regions.

The availability of social media and collaborative technology tools have enabled those of us in what has been the loneliest position in any district, to establish connections throughout the country and build trusting relationships with those facing the same challenges and opportunities. Trusting the professional judgment of the person providing an insight, recommendation, or advice allows connected superintendents to move more quickly, respond more effectively, and be overall more nimble than our predecessors.

The impact of what Covey calls "The Speed of Trust" is on display through every Twitter chat and Voxer thread in which I participate. While the challenges of educational leadership continue to evolve, many of the solutions to the specific challenges that each of us face have already been identified in districts across the country who have already been forced to tackle any given issue.

As with any field where technology advancements take place, the initial application can be clunky and be enough of an obstacle to keep all but the most tech savvy from changing practice. The tools available today to help leaders learn with and from this network of trusted peers are so intuitive and easy, that they just fade into the background. Users can be up to speed on the device or application in a few minutes and then fully engage in the content of the conversation focusing on the specific challenge or circumstance that they are addressing.

Examples of this phenomenon benefitting me personally in my present district run the gamut from being able to collaborate with colleagues across the country on topics ranging from exploring full-day kindergarten to responding to the death of a student, from going 1:1 to exploring the benefits of a professional development network, and the list will go on.

While I still highly value my strong local network of superintendents from whom I learn a lot about leading in the context, I, and consequently my district, would not be making nearly as much progress toward our mission if it were not for the benefits of using the tools of the twenty-first century to connect with an innovative and diverse network of trusted peers.

Chapter Two

Unlearning Planning and Change Process

Every organization must be prepared to abandon everything it does to survive in the future.

—Peter Drucker

Reflection Questions

Do you think that leaders should wait and observe for a year before making changes?
Have you successfully implemented change?
In what ways do you measure system or initiative effectiveness?

Stop-Think-Act

With whom in your organization do you plan for future growth?
What steps are taken when an initiative is selected?
What is your plan for next year? Next week? Tomorrow?
Write down an outline for planning with people, process, outcomes, and measures.

PHILOSOPHY OF CHANGE: WHY CHANGE?

Throughout the world, public schools still resemble, in many ways, the nineteenth-century industrial factory model. In a 2006 article in *Time* magazine, there is commentary on what would happen if Rip Van Winkle appeared in the twenty-first century (see excerpt below): "The world has changed, but the American classroom, for the most part, hasn't. Now educators are starting to look at what must be done to make sure our kids make the grade in the new global economy."

> "There's a dark little joke exchanged by educators with a dissident streak: Rip Van Winkle awakens in the 21st century after a hundred-year snooze and is, of course, utterly bewildered by what he sees. Men and women dash about, talking to small metal devices pinned to their ears. Young people sit at home on sofas, moving miniature athletes around on electronic screens. Older folk defy death and disability with metronomes in their chests and with hips made of metal and plastic. Airports, hospitals, shopping malls—every place Rip goes just baffles him. But when he finally walks into a schoolroom, the old ..." Read more: How to Bring Our Schools Out of the 20th Century—TIME. By: Claudia Wallis and Sonja Steptoe Sunday, Dec. 10, 2006, http://content.time.com/time/magazine/article/0,9171,1568480,00.html#ixzz2nEWV6tl2.

The point of the article is that Rip Van Winkle is confused by modern day experiences like airplanes, shopping malls, electronics, etc.—but when he walks into a classroom he is calm and comfortable ... because structurally speaking, most classrooms have not changed (or had not changed as of 2006). The same can be said in many places in 2017 too. Van Winkle did not have to unlearn conceptual design of schools since the structures remained, and in many instances still remain, stagnant.

A fundamental shift, or an unlearning paradigm, is what we see taking place in select schools around the country. Whether it's a forward thinking public school in a suburban, urban, or rural area, a special charter school, High Tech High School in San Diego, CA, or a selective enrollment magnet school in Chicago, fundamental shifts in design, choice, leadership, and organization are taking place. Why do schools still operate as they did in the nineteenth century? Why do rows and bells and separate courses designed by the Committee of Ten in 1892 still perpetuate and permeate our society?

Thought leaders and intellectuals like Sir Ken Robinson and Dr. John Hattie are sharing, writing, communicating, and challenging contemporary constructs of school as well as institutional practices and norms in schooling. Robinson calls for a shift in the paradigm of the industrial age and Hattie's meta-analyses call into question commonly held beliefs and practices.

Hattie's findings also shed light on what many already know: feedback is king (or queen) in terms of impacting learning for both students and adults (Hattie and Yates, 2014, p. 69).

Our premise in the *Unlearning Leader: Leading for Tomorrow's Schools Today* is that commonly held beliefs must give way, or be *unlearned*, to make room for uncommon beliefs and practices. As mentioned in the Preface, the colors of the yield sign have changed yet many in the audience at workshops still raise their hands when asked if they believe the yield sign colors are yellow and black instead of red and white.

Many, including us, were taught, and we learned, that yield signs were yellow and black, yet they we "knew" they were red and white. They used to be yellow and black so it proves quite difficult to unlearn a seemingly simple concept.

Like the colors of the yield sign, so too are commonly held beliefs about leading and managing adults, schools, and students. It's time to unlearn—those who can unlearn are reaping huge benefits in all fields. We submit that Google unlearned how to select talented employees. Instead of relying on the belief that experience and education are the effective predictors of success at work, Google chose to focus on talent.

We submit that Apple unlearned how a telephone operates. Apple also helped society, billions of people, unlearn the definition of the word "tablet." Apple helped society unlearn by "thinking differently." These major shifts in the world are recent. It's no surprise that more than a half billion people are on Facebook. Society as a whole is unlearning how to connect and form relationships.

Unlearning how to connect, communicate, relate, and live is all around us. Schools and school system leaders need to unlearn their own experiences in school so that a new future can be created for the world's children. The exciting part about leading change is that the results cascade like a pebble tossed into the stream; the ripples move far beyond the starting point and the momentum grows and grows. The unlearning leader is taking risks and making bold leaps of courage to ensure that tomorrow's schools are better aligned with the needs of the future.

The point of course is that educational leaders have a charge to prepare students for schooling, work, and life in their future, not the past of the leaders and policy makers. So, while nostalgia fans might want their kids' schooling to look like their own, our charge as leaders is to foster innovative, modern, present day, future-focused learning organizations! Yesterday may have been groovy and keen, but it's over. Today is grand, and it's here that we live. Tomorrow should be something new and better, and for that we unlearn and recreate.

Thankfully there are amazing teachers, students, support staff, administrators, board members, and community members in many public school districts and these lofty goals can be and have been realized! It's incumbent upon leaders to unlearn the culturally and historically ingrained models of schools, schooling, and classroom set up that have permeated the American schools since the 1800s.

It really is time to unlearn the factory model of public schooling. Industrial revolutionary ideas served society well for many years, and now their time has passed. The time is now to create and envision information age schools and an information age society. The time is now to unlearn that the Committee of Ten is right forever. The time is now to unlearn that bells and 40 minute units of time in isolation best "teaches" content. It's time to unlearn the structures that exist in school.

In 2017, seven years past the birth of Apple's iPad, and 19 years since Google was founded, workspaces in schools should be different to reflect the environments of these two successful companies. We have engaged in significant design and space change endeavors in our respective systems. We have unlearned the 25–30 desks in symmetrical rows with the teacher at the head of the class model. We are working to help members of our organizations also unlearn this construct.

Why should the cinder block walls in schools resemble the walls in hospitals and prisons? Why should classrooms be closed boxes living in isolation from one another? Why should a child spend 13 years thinking that each subject or topic exists in isolation for 40–60 minutes at a time? Why change? Because the needs for the rest of the world are changing. Because all that used to exist in a print textbook is found on the Internet and literally in the palms of our hands. Because the exponential changes around us need to permeate the seemingly impermeable walls of the public school system. Why change? Because Alvin Toeffler was correct and prophetic when he penned the famous quote: *The illiterate of the 21st century will not be those who cannot read and write, but those who cannot learn, unlearn, and relearn.*

In addition, we believe that the five-year strategic plan model must be unlearned. Modeled after Stalin's creation in 1928, the five-year strategic plan is no longer relevant, as if it ever was relevant. Especially with the rapid rates of change in our world, global economy, technology, and research findings, who can wait five years for a change and who can accurately plan education or other needs five years out?

We entered systems where binder after binder of plan after plan neatly filled in the bookshelves in our offices. Change, though, does not fill any neatly ordered book shelf. Change, timely change, has been largely absent in school systems. We want to walk the talk and through unlearning, lead and move our organizations forward.

DON'T GET STUCK IN THE PLANNING PHASE

Edwards Deming proffers the Plan Do Study Act (PDSA) system: "The PDSA Cycle is a systematic series of steps for gaining valuable learning and knowledge for the continual improvement of a product or process. Also known as the Deming Wheel, or Deming Cycle, the concept and application were first introduced to Dr. Deming by his mentor, Walter Shewhart of the famous Bell Laboratories in New York." Retrieved from: https://www.deming.org/theman/theories/pdsacycle.

When Mike arrived in Deerfield there were many thoughtful plans: the Strategic Plan from 2011, the Master Facilities Plan from 2012, and others. It was a very well planned district. The challenges that the new leadership team faced were contained in the fact that the district was stuck in Plan mode. They did not have the execution of plans in their wheelhouse. The district was stuck.

With a stroke of luck, good timing, and a lot of well-crafted plans guiding their work, the new board tasked the new superintendent and the new leadership team to move from Plan to Do. Unlearning in this system took many forms. The culture and processes that stymied action had to be unlearned by everyone. Essentially the board tasked the team to unlearn that which seemed to stifle change.

We believe the unlearning leadership team has to do things a little bit differently than in a traditional leadership team. In Deerfield, for example, the preceding 4 years have resulted in major changes for students, staff, and community under PDSA. That district has moved from planning to doing, studying, acting, refining the planning, doing some more, enhancing the study phase, and then acting even more.

Many leadership training programs and experts state that what is expected is measured and what is tolerated is promoted. In this system, part of the unlearning also involved survey collection. From organizational culture, climate, academic performance, and others, the district started to collect data on what its stated purposes were. The system unlearned not acting by starting to put their money where its mouth was and by beginning to inspect what they stated they respected.

As reference to the power of unlearning and the impact that unlearning had on the Deerfield Public Schools, see one of Mike's blog posts on the changes that took place and impacted students, staff, and community in the Deerfield Public Schools:

We continue to embark on ways to improve learning opportunities for students, staff, leaders and members of our community. The upcoming school year 2015-2016 will focus on full day kindergarten, enhanced science curricular resources for all students in grades K–5, completely renovated science lab classrooms for all students in grades 6–8, elective choice for 8th grade students, instrumental music during the school day, and so much more! Stay tuned as we highlight our continued innovative approaches to learning and teaching.

The listing of accomplishments in a 36-month period for this public school system is long and unusual. The entire organization of nearly 500 adult employees on behalf of 3,000 students from grades PK–8 worked in unison to accomplish major organizational change in a public school system. They unlearned the realities of the past that held them up. Yes, it was true, for example, that several years ago it was believed that available space was an issue preventing full-day kindergarten.

Yet an unlearning approach, one that activated the shared vision for full-day kindergarten helped the system go from a planning phase to a doing phase in three months! Initial studies of the impact of the kindergarten program, for example, are highly supportive of the change. PDSA is powerful, as Deming learned and shared, when all component parts are enacted.

Many suggest that it is a greater challenge to motivate teachers in an already high performing system to change. Yet in this system, through inspiring a shared vision, challenging the process, and enabling others to act, three of the five exemplary practices of leadership, major movement took place on behalf of students, staff, and community in a relatively short period of time. A quote that summarizes the change process is found in Bullis et al. (2016b):

> We accomplished this by using a holistic school improvement planning process that utilized the power and collective capacity of student, staff, parent, and community voice. Working under an intensive, two-year Plan-Do-Study-Act process, principal leadership transformed student learning and school facilities for decades to come. (53)

With a concentrated series of approaches grounded in research, resource, planning, and drive, in Deerfield they did what many never thought possible. They rebuilt the culture, climate, and vision. They focused on Engage, Inspire, Empower as a motto, a mission, a vision, and a rallying cry for leadership, change, education, and joy.

MISSION/VISION

Immediately after starting as the superintendent in Deerfield, Mike asked every administrator in the leadership team to share the mission of the district. No one was able to recite that mission statement; the one that was created two years prior to the question, so the leadership team opted to embrace the three main action verbs. Engage, Inspire, Empower. This essentially became the mission/vision/motto for the district.

Every action, statement, speech, communication, business card, etc., would have the words Engage, Inspire, Empower. Every initiative, plan, program, proposal would be held to the standards of engaging, inspiring, and empowering those responsible and those impacted.

As leaders they were modeling the way, inspiring a shared vision, and it was working. The adoption and acceptance of the streamlined mission was actually quite easy since multiple stakeholders created the mission statement in the first place. And although very few remembered what they agreed to, nearly all remembered and respected the three action verbs! In essence the magnitude of changes challenged the process.

In the organization there were many plans and goals, and dreams. There was an abundance of "Plan" and "Study" and a shortage of "Do" and "Act." The leadership team, focused on the renewed energy of mission and vision, brought elements of those plans to life. The leadership unlearned plan, plan, study, plan, plan, study. The leadership team, with the vision of the board and the mission of the board began to DO and ACT.

The 2011 Strategic Plan (yes, a five-year plan) contained lofty and honorable mission and vision statements:

Mission: Provide educational experiences of the highest quality that Engage, Inspire, and Empower each student to excel and contribute in a changing world.

Vision: District 109 students will excel and contribute when they have the knowledge and skills to be:

- Lifelong, self-directed learners
- Critical and creative thinkers
- Effective communicators
- Collaborative team members
- Respectful and responsible members of society

The leadership team needed to unlearn the concept that all of those words equaled change and progress. They needed to unlearn that a plan must be made by consensus. They unlearned that everyone's contributions needed to be recorded so everyone felt good. The good feelings gave way to frustration when the clarity of focus and purpose was absent.

The reality is, no matter how lofty those words were, no one knew what they said! The distillation into three words—Engage, Inspire, Empower— made far more sense. They unlearned the five-year plan and they learned three words. They unlearned making everyone feel good and they learned to lead with input and not with consensus.

They started with getting the right people on the bus and then they drove the bus. They unlearned long-held concepts and beliefs. They opened their minds and hearts with renewed possibility. They unlearned that leadership rested with position. They learned leaders were all around them.

Similarly, at Leyden, the district also had a mission statement that was on the walls and on the website, but lacking any action. In fact, no one in the district was able to recite their mission statement from memory either. So Nick decided to lead the district towards strategic planning.

In the interest of unlearning traditional strategic planning, the district decided they did not want to create a binder. Instead they wanted a strategic plan that would fit on one page and be simple and actionable for everyone in the district. During the summer of 2016, stakeholders representing students, teachers, support staff, administrators, board members, and local business leaders gathered with a facilitator to establish a mission statement, a vision statement, and some brief, actionable district goals.

After three days of meetings the mission statement was changed from "Leyden District 212 supports a community of lifelong learners who prepare for global change, respect diversity, accept personal responsibility, and pursue a sense of fulfillment" to "Educate–Enrich–Empower: Students and Communities." Twenty-five words became six words and now every stakeholder at Leyden is able to speak the same language about the district's mission.

For a vision, the strategic planning team adopted the motto of the Board of Education, "Doing What's Best for the Kids." In that simple phrase, the district is committed to be flexible into the future. As the needs of students continue to evolve and change, the district is committing to evolve also as they always do what's best for the kids.

INSPIRE A SHARED VISION
(SIDEBAR—MID-CHAPTER FEATURE)

The second exemplary practice shown by effective leaders according to the findings of Kouzes and Posner is *Inspire a Shared Vision*. With this exemplary practice of leadership, the admired and effective leaders "enlist others in a common vision by appealing to shared aspirations." Common strategic planning exercises contain a mission/vision development sequence.

The key is to develop a plan that makes sense, reflects common ideals and vision, and can actually be executed.

> People want leaders who are upbeat, optimistic, and positive about the future. It's really the only way you can get people to willingly follow you to someplace they have never been before. (p. 151)

When we arrived in our respective organizations there were established mission and vision statements. But those statements were not reflective of inspired visions or reflective of collective reality.

Both of us enlisted our teammates, our own leadership vision, the goals and aspirations of the Boards of Education, and through deliberate, intentional practice, we each are working to Inspire a Shared Vision. Leaders who get the entire organization to be able to speak the words that represent the organization are showing results of the Inspire a Shared Vision practice. In Deerfield with #Engage109 on Twitter and their mantra of Engage, Inspire, Empower, everyone knows that all they do is under the umbrella of those verbs and concepts.

At Leyden, doing what's best for kids, as described in this chapter, took twenty-six words and distilled them into six. It's not the word count that inspires, it is through the process and the actions accompanying the process that serve as the inspiration. Both districts' results continue to show sustained results and actions that align with their inspired and shared visions.

As Himebaugh and Lubelfeld (2016) shared in a journal article about the inspired shared vision experiences in Deerfield:

Concentrating on six broad areas of concern: social emotional learning, fine arts, Science, Technology, Engineering and Math (STEM), gifted/tracking, world languages, and exploratory programming, the 140 member community task force set out to prove what a dedicated group of individuals could do on behalf of the public schools. Each of the six middle school administrators plus central office leaders led a subcommittee, and joined with students, teachers, parents, and community members to put vision into action. We put thoughts into practice, all under the broad umbrella of **Engage, Inspire, Empower**. These subcommittees were composed of students, teachers, community members as well as leadership team representatives.

In order to live out these shared visions and to get things done, as Collins writes in *Good to Great*, "You need to get the right people on the right seats on the bus" (13). As is described in the next section, selection of staff, inspiring a shared vision and effectuating it can be accomplished with the right teams and the right teammates.

SELECTION OF STAFF: CHANGE IN PROCESS

As Sanfelippo and Sinanis state on page 95 of their book *Hacking Leadership*: "The US Department of Education Statistics reports that nearly 17 percent of teachers leave the classroom in their first five years (2015)."

Hiring superstars, as they state as Hack 7, is exactly what the authors have been doing in their various leadership posts.

From a leadership perspective, the team of building and district administrators in the Deerfield Public Schools began their journey with a deliberate and intentional focus on selection of staff. They unlearned old practices with a shared vision. They unlearned previously in place laissez-faire approaches to staff selection by learning focused, deliberate, and disciplined selection of staff processes grounded in research and implemented with fidelity.

Several years prior to the new administration, building leaders were trained on structured selection tools. The training was good, everyone was excited, but then there were no structures or systems in place and the training fell to the wayside.

As Collins writes in *Good to Great*, it's essential to confront the brutal facts yet never lose faith (65) for the organization to move forward. In the fashion of the great companies about which Collins writes and through the lens of the MICEE practices distilled from Kouzes and Posner's years of research and publishing, they started the journey with a focus on people.

In Deerfield they confronted the brutal facts that their training never impacted systems, structures, or change. Therefore, under new leadership they unlearned old ways for improvement and so far, it is a formula that works. It's second order change where structures, systems, approaches, and discipline are now the norm for the staff selection process.

The focus on a new process for the selection of staff began the administration's new reality of operating as a team under unifying structures. Unlearning required them to accept change as real, not just with lip service and compliance, but with real ownership. The reality is some never did this and they realized that organization was not for them anymore and they moved on. Unlearn that everyone needs to stay in their positions just because that's the way it's always been done (more on this concept in the next chapter).

Other leaders embraced the changes in focus, discipline, and leadership over a period of one, two, or three years. The key point here is that the leadership unled the leadership team in processes and procedures in staff selection that had been in place for years as a bold starting point for meaningful change.

Structured selection instruments/interviews allow leaders to manage the thousands of active applications in job application databases. This process is reflected in Kouzes and Posner's findings that Empowering Others to Act is another of the five main practices of exemplary leadership. All of the leadership falls under the umbrella framework of MICEE.

In terms of staff selection, Deerfield Public School District 109 trains administrators on staff selection and leadership development using evidence-based practices. The research upon which these practices are based comes from nearly a century of research from organizational psychology. The search for excellence has science to back up the process and work. With fidelity to the process, with structured selection as well as resume review, essay review, and fit interviews with input teams, practitioners can predict, with up to 88 percent (0.88) certainty that their chosen candidate will be excellent in the particular role.

Based on reports from Schmidt and Hunter, the structured interview process helps increase this validity (of accuracy of selection of staff) by between 0.23 and 0.50. As a contrast, a selection process without scientifically-based interview instruments like those found in traditional unstructured selection yields about a 30 percent (0.30) predictive validity.

Taking that 0.30 and adding the value of structured interviews (0.51), reference checks (0.26), and valuing the training and experience of candidates (0.11), the whole process takes that traditional 30 and moves it up to a structured 88! For more sources from the US Government Office of Personnel Management, visit: http://apps.opm.gov/ADT/Content.aspx?page=RelatedDocuments.

While no staff selection system is perfect, leaders who use evidence-based structured selection systems are proud of implementation of the selection and development of talent at all levels. The staff selected under these evidence-based practices include staff in administrative roles, frontline support personnel, teaching staff, etc. Leaders have high expectations for all students, all staff, all administrators, all vendors, all partners, and everyone with whom they work.

With leadership, fidelity, training, support, and accountability measures, the unlearning turns into new practices and the organization changes. Through the disciplined, possibly even rigid, selection processes the leadership team unlearned years of rules, expectations, procedures, protocols, and experiences that had not moved the organization from Plan to Do. The new selection of staff format unified the leadership team.

The systemic application of new rules set in motion many additional second order changes that will impact learners and the community for decades. This was a visible change and a visible shift. Unlearning the concept that prior experience and education yielded the best teachers was not easy. It is taking years to change some people's minds. Following the lead of Google and others, it's talent and talent selection that makes all the difference in selection of staff. Equipping the leadership with these tools requires an unlearning leader.

One of the cornerstones of the unlearning leader is building relationships, as highlighted later in the book, relationships are built upon trust and trust is everything. We're reminded of a quote from successful Southwest Airlines founder Herb Kelleher: "You have to treat your employees like customers."

In addition to changes in the selection of staff process, unlearning the old ways and changing, Deerfield also put measures and metrics in place to inspect what they respected. Organizational culture, climate, student engagement, transformation efforts, and general satisfaction are regularly measured with surveys, interviews, and focus groups. The leadership team started to gather baseline data and then they began measuring year after year, to see growth, trends, and impacts.

INNOVATION IN PRACTICE

George Couros's book *The Innovator's Mindset*, challenges traditional thinking about innovation, change, and impact. According to Couros:

> Change can be hard and sometimes seemingly insurmountable, but remember, *change is an opportunity to do something amazing.* If we embrace this mindset and become the innovators our kids need (and need to be), the opportunities in front of us are endless. (10)

The story for Deerfield about progressing from being stuck in the Plan phase to evolving into a Plan Do Study Act organization started in August 2013. At the August 2013 Institute Day when during the superintendent's introductory remarks, he referenced an Innovation Grant process for trailblazing teachers, the institute day itself became an example of unlearning. No one could remember the last time the entire district staff assembled together as a unified group. No one could remember the last time the superintendent called for innovation.

The new leadership team created a new reality of unifying the entire faculty and staff at the start of the year. Everyone would learn together. Everyone would hear the same unifying messages. As mentioned, the streamlined motto of Engage, Inspire, Empower, the main verbs from the existing mission statement, would guide the work of the district. This would start with an Innovation Grant competition. Unlearning on a large scale started.

The district started the innovation grant competition in October 2013, for those "trailblazer teachers" who wanted to experiment with a 1:1 learning environment as a pilot before the district ultimately decided to become a 1:1 school system in March 2014. The district had studied 1:1 for many years yet there had been no tangible plans or action toward this large-scale implementation. Like Couros states "Designing solutions with both the individuals' interests and the end goal in mind is crucial for any innovation to be successful" (26).

The district was committed to Engage, Inspire, Empower its students, staff, and community. They were about to literally put their money where their mission was. The first phase of the innovation grant pilot was about so much more than providing devices, it was about transforming teaching and learning concepts. It was about providing students and teachers with access to resources and technology at their fingertips to facilitate creativity, innovation, collaboration, global awareness, information literacy, and media literacy. This truly was an opportunity to do amazing things!

Organizationally it was about unlearning control. No longer would the mandates and edicts come from external sources, instead, the trailblazers would inform the system. The trailblazers would experiment and impact the curriculum and instruction and inform the system. The collaborative approaches would become the norm. They started as novelty.

Teachers would choose their own course of action with guidance from the administration. This defined autonomy reflected a new culture of collaboration. This was an organizational unlearning process that integrated many leadership principles and moved the organization from being stuck at the planning phase in so many areas to an organization that did, studied, and acted on all fronts. Second order change was happening!

At Leyden the district utilizes a somewhat typical Professional Learning Community (PLC) model with weekly late starts for students on Wednesday mornings. During this time, departments meet to review curriculum, plan, develop assessments, and more. In an effort to unlearn and expand the PLC model, Leyden created the opportunity for a group of teachers to opt-in to an alternative PLC group called the Innovation Incubators.

This interdisciplinary group of teachers meets during the regular Wednesday morning time. Their focus is experimentation, creativity, and innovation. They were told to think differently, try things, and make recommendations to the administration. In 2015, they began creating an idea to create a "school within a school" that focuses on project-based learning. They were given the time and flexibility to think differently, and now, their creation will soon become a reality.

Educators need to let go of the thought that ideas come from administrators and teachers enact the change. When administrators unlearn top-down leadership and trust the ideas and the hard work of their teachers, exciting things can happen. Very soon, a group of Leyden students will be able to access a completely new educational experience. That will be possible because leaders gave time, resources, and trust to their staff.

By DOing transformation as opposed to the normal, planning, discussing, forming committee after committee, and making reports to the board and superintendent, the new leadership focus challenged the process and ACTed. Both districts put into place an empowerment of teachers and students. The teachers, students, parents, and all stakeholders were asked for input and opinion about the pedagogical shifts.

They then were able to plan for larger scale deployment and study the *what* and *how* while always staying connected to the *why*! Kouzes and Posner found that *Challenge the Process* is one of the five exemplary practices of leadership.

In the Leyden example there was a shift, or unlearning of the command control from administration to a more collaborative approach. The unlearning leader shifts approaches based upon time, need, and impact. The four Cs: communication, collaboration, critical thinking, and creativity are for students and adults! Unlearning adult centric decision-making impacts students, staff, and community in many lasting ways.

SUMMARY

As a recap, the learning purposes of this book include:

- Energize people to think, act, and do leadership differently.
- Embody an innovative mindset at all levels that supports unlearning.
- Model and share through experience, observation, and trial and error a new way of leading from within the organization.

The examples shared from the leadership approaches reflect and show actual practical situations where people were energized to think, act, and do leadership differently. The mindset clearly was and still is innovative. Like Couros states in *The Innovator's Mindset*:

> In reality, you can't make anyone change; people can only change themselves. What you can do is create the conditions where change is more likely to happen. As a leader, you can create those conditions by taking a strength-based approach for learning and leadership and unleashing talent in your organization. (Couros, 2016)

During the 1:1 pilot period in Deerfield from December 2013 through June 2014 the District conducted surveys of grant winning teachers, their students, and the student's parents.

Quotes from the Teacher Survey—1:1 Innovation Grant Teachers:

What has been the best part of the pilot so far for your class?

> I love the fact that my students are able to access the internet, Google, apps, etc. easily. When we didn't have 1:1 Chromebooks, it took a lot of time to go to the Chromebook cart and distribute the Chromebooks. It also took a lot of time to put each Chromebook back in the cart. Valuable instructional time was lost. Now, the students can easily log into the Chromebooks to complete assignments. We no longer miss valuable instructional time.

The amount of work that is produced has increased and the pride that students take in creating and learning new things that are more meaningful to them.

I am amazed at how the technology supports student self-directedness and student-driven instruction. I find that the kids sometimes come up with better ideas with this technology at their fingertips. As a result, we have a much more collaborative classroom than before!

What else would you like to share with us about the 1:1 pilot?

Some of the things that I thought might be an issue have not been. Students have not been forgetting their computers. We've seldom had to charge one in class. No breakage so far, either! We need Hapara, however, as I really need to be able to monitor what my students are doing during Guided Reading when I am with a small group and they are working independently.

Student Quotes:

What has been the best part of the 1:1 pilot so far for you or your class/team?

I like being able to have our own computers to do extra math and stuff like that on it. It's also fun that when I get home from school I get to write stories on Google drive.

The best part of having a 1:1 Chromebooks are that you get to have fun with your homework.

I enjoy using our Chromebooks for science and writing. In writing we can type instead of print which lets me do it ten times faster. In science we use a science website with videos which is also really fun and a MUCH better learning experience.

Since I have 3 other brothers that also need to get homework done and only 1 computer at home the Chromebook has allowed me to get my homework finished earlier.

I can show my parents what I'm doing and I have a personal device at home.

Parent Survey Quotes:

What has been the best part of the 1:1 pilot so far for your child?

She is so proud and confident that she's been empowered with this technology. She loves the new apps and asks to fill downtime at home playing with it—way better than zoning out with TV when she needs quiet time.

My 1st grader is able to be challenged and also enjoy doing the learning, because he thinks it is playing games

The ability to easily discuss what my child is doing throughout the school day and if there is confusion or changes to be made, I can assist and changes can easily be made in real time.

Also, teachers are able to make comments in real time and students can make corrections before submitting work.

After three months of intense review and Innovation Grant implementation of transformative one-to-one learning environments in forty pilot classrooms the administration made a recommendation to the Board of Education for full implementation of one-to-one for the 2014–2015 school year starting in August 2014.

In chapter 3, readers will unlearn teacher-centered and adult-focused leadership and organization. With the learner agency and student empowerment in place at the Leyden High Schools, the reader will learn how students can be integrated into learning, teaching, operations, planning, and powerful second order changes.

In chapter 2, you learned about effective and impactful change case studies. You read that our nation's public schools still resemble, in many ways, the nineteenth-century industrial factory model. In a 2006 Time magazine article, there was an anecdote about how Rip Van Winkle awakens and feels right at home in a school. The point of course is that our charge as leaders is to prepare students for schooling and work in THEIR future.

Our charge is also to foster innovative, modern, present day, future-focused learning organizations! Through deliberate and disciplined leadership and structures, any organization can replicate the case study examples shared in the chapter. In chapter 2, you learned how to unlearn the change quagmire and "do" paradox present in many organizations. As we move on to chapter 3, you will learn how unlearning acceptance of the status quo can make multiple changes.

S—Stop and reflect on the main ideas of the chapter. What are your metrics for measuring successful change initiatives? What staff selection processes are in place for the organization. Do leaders apply science or "gut" for staff selection?

U—Understand—Does your community have an understanding of why you are doing what you are doing?

P—Plan for how you will lead, support, define, or engage in changes for improvement.

T—Think of some take-aways from this chapter you will act on and do.

Chat: Pick an edchat, like #TEDedChat, where participants discusses TED Talks, TED-Ed Lessons & education—ed.ted.com. This chat takes place weekly on Tuesdays from 6:00 pm to 7:00 pm CDT. If you have not yet done this—now is the time to experience a digital form of professional development.

PRACTITIONER COMMENTARY— ANDRE SPENCER

Dr. Andre Spencer is the superintendent of the 11,000 student Harrison School District 2 in Colorado Springs, Colorado.

Change is inevitable. Change has to be the driver of K–12 education in an ever-changing globally connected world. Superintendents must have a vision for change. Without a doubt, the development of technology brings about such connectedness, which creates the need for change.

If our schools and scholars are going to be globally competitive, we must change the ways in which we implement and measure teaching and learning. As President Barack Obama stated, "Change will not come if we wait for some other person or some other time. We are the ones we've been waiting for. We are the change that we seek." Superintendents of schools in America, must be the ones to reflect the change in education that we wish to see. If not now, then when … if not us, then whom.

When change is successfully implemented, it requires continuous relationship development. It is imperative that superintendents of schools understand the importance of constructing and sustaining relationships with adults and scholars. Relationships must honestly promote trust, core-values, and authenticity.

Superintendents must demonstrate the wherewithal in their ability to identify the appropriate stakeholders to engage in order to promote everlasting success for all scholars. If change does not include relationship development, the change will not be sustained over time.

It is essential that superintendents intentionally build quality relationships with scholars, educators, parents, board members, community, politicians, and other stakeholders. Superintendents must openly and honestly communicate the need for change through the lens of improving outcomes for scholars and their changing communities.

Nonetheless, the change must be innovative. It is important for superintendents to share the honest challenges with change. Consequently, when trusting relationships are developed, the message becomes more credible. It is important for superintendents to recognize the connectedness between vision, change, innovation, and relationships. When the connectedness is well-balanced, achievement is foreseeable.

Comprehensibly, change is hard, but change is possible. However, change without vision, innovation, and trusting relationships, is practically impossible. Relationships are relevant to change academic outcomes. As Teddy Roosevelt once said, "Children do not care how much you know until they know how much you care." Superintendents must lead the way to building healthy relationships with scholars by ensuring access and opportunity for all.

When superintendents promote the significance of engaging in teaching and learning through the lens of building relationships by organizing innovative learning experiences threaded with rigorous content and relevant connections to the lives of scholars—educators will ultimately see the improvements in K–12 education that is expected.

Figure 2.1   Increase Achievement Process Model.

As educators, if superintendents are sincere about closing the achievement gaps, they will focus on equity and opportunity gaps, while cultivating relationships that promote innovative teaching and learning. This paradigm shift in K–12 education must start now. Although there is a sincere need for urgency in K–12 education, superintendents must perform high levels of vision and change planning, while preventing educational paralysis.

Undoubtedly, superintendents of schools must have an established framework for implementing change, which incorporates innovative best practices. This happens when superintendents create networks of superintendents (e.g., Voxer, Twitter, AASA, etc.) to engage in dialogue. These superintendent cohorts cultivate valuable conversations and relationships, which will ultimately change the way in which teaching and learning occurs in American schools.

Everyone is aware that educational outcomes in America are under tough scrutiny. If superintendents do not have a clear vision to implement change with innovative practices and maintain quality relationships, achievement will suffer. Figure 2.1 is a visual representation of the impact of the connectedness.

Undoubtedly, change in American K–12 education must occur. However, sustainable change is impossible when vision, innovation, and relationships are non-existent. Vision, change, innovation, and relationships are the mechanisms needed to bring about improvements in achievement in K–12 education. If either construct is missing, improvements will not be possible. Superintendents—Our scholars are depending on us.

The time for change is now!

Chapter Three

Unlearning "That's the Way We Have Always Done It"

I would rather die of passion than of boredom.

—Vincent van Gogh

Reflection Questions

What are typical obstructions to change in school systems?
Why is leading differently so often halted or stymied by "tradition?"
What actionable techniques lead to meaningful and lasting change?

Stop-Think-Act

What major points are resonating with you at this point in the book? How have you experienced unlearning leadership?
Think about the need for unlearning in your current organization—what should you unlearn first?
Act on rejecting the stifling concept of "That's the way we've always done it."

NO MORE STATUS QUO

In the world of sales, it's often said that the customer is always right. Corporate leaders spend countless hours and dollars doing market research to determine what consumers want and need. In both examples, specific attention is given to the end users. Schools, however, often ignore their end users, namely students. In education, the teacher has always been the "Sage on the Stage." That's the way we've always done it.

Keeping things the way they have always been is often the easy thing to do. Adults (educators, parents, and community members) are comfortable when the education of today's youth looks mostly like the education they received themselves when they were younger. These stakeholders consider themselves experts on education as a result of having been educated themselves.

Consider the members of your Board of Education. Perhaps they have been looking at education through the lens of their children's experiences for years. Maybe their students have long left the system. It can be difficult to have those particular elected officials unlearn their long-held beliefs about what is right and correct in education. It's often challenging for a school leader to get support for change, even though the change might be needed, due to the inability of others to unlearn.

The unlearning leader needs to teach others, including the other adults in the organization, what, how, why, and when to unlearn. The past conditions that allowed students to thrive in education and in life are different now. Change is constant in terms of research, evidence, and experience. It's incumbent upon us all to open ourselves up to unlearning.

Those same adults would likely agree that the world is changing and that our current students face a different future, one that is difficult for us to predict. Ian Jukes and Ted McCain illustrated the power of "That's the Way We've Always Done It" in a 2007 article, "Reconsidering Education in the Information & Communication Age." They offered the following perspective on the history of our railroad system:

Today in the United States, the spacing between the rails on railroad tracks is always 4 feet, 8 1/2 inches—a rather odd and seemingly arbitrary number. Why is that particular spacing always used? Because that's the rail spacing they used to build the railroads in England, and English expatriates built the U.S. railroads.

Why did the English use that particular spacing? Because the same people built horse-drawn wagons in the pre-railroad era, and that's the axle width wagon makers who built the first railroad cars used.

Why did the wagon makers use that particular axle width? They did this because, if they used any other axle spacing, the wagon wheels would break on the sides of the established wheel ruts.

So, where did those old rutted roads come from? The first long distance roads in Britain and Europe were built by Imperial Rome for the use of the Roman military, and they have been in use ever since.

Why did the Romans use that particular axle spacing? Roman war chariots formed the initial ruts in these first roads, and everyone ever since has had to adapt to those ruts to avoid destroying their wheels. Thus the United States standard railroad track spacing of 4 feet, 8 1/2 inches derives from the original specification for an Imperial Roman war chariot.

What this all means: Specifications, bureaucracies, institutions, and systems have a natural tendency to solidify in their ways, requiring people to do things the same way they have traditionally been done. This, despite the fact the world is changing around us all the time. In this situation, you might find yourself sometimes asking, "What horse's ass came up with this way of doing things?" In the case of the railways, you would be closer to the truth than you imagined, because the Imperial Roman war chariots were made just wide enough to accommodate two horses asses.

Indeed, a horse's ass did originally determine the way we do some things now, and we finally have the answer to the original question. And there's more.

There's new twist to the story about railroad track spacing and horses' behinds. When we see a space shuttle sitting on its launch pad, there are two big booster rockets attached to the sides of the main fuel tank. These are solid rocket boosters, or SRBs, which are made at the ATK Thiokol Propulsion factory in Utah. The engineers who designed the SRBs might have preferred to make them a bit fatter, but the SRBs have to be shipped by train from the factory in Utah to the launch site in Florida. The railroad line from the factory runs through various tunnels in the mountains. The tunnels are slightly wider than the railroad track, and the railroad track is about as wide as two horses' behinds.

So, a major design feature of what is arguably the world's most advanced transportation system was determined over 2,000 years ago by the width of a horse's ass!

When you consider this story in the context of our current modern educational system, the similarities are disturbing. Why do we take 3 months off in the summertime? Why do we organize desks into rows and columns? Why do we split our curriculum up into separate departments and separate courses? Are any of these best practices or ... The Way We've Always Done It?

We all need to overcome the normal tendency toward the way things have always been done, our school districts need to adopt a different mentality. We need to cultivate a culture of innovation and change. In essence, we need to unlearn the old ways. In order to do this, leadership needs to confront the brutal facts and hold some tough conversations.

This requires a degree of organizational humility, where your district acknowledges that they may not have all of the answers and the current practices may be wrong. However, they need to be willing to make iterative changes, be flexible and nimble, and take responsible risks to better meet the needs of their students. This path contains failures, criticism, and other road-blocks, but this is the only path that will allow us to move forward. Recall the need to create a safe culture where fail means first attempt at learning as was discussed in chapter 1.

Back to horses, former AASA Superintendent of the Year, Mark Edwards, once told us that change is possible in education. He said, "If we are not capable of change in education, we would be teaching drivers' education on horseback." As the world changes, we have a responsibility to adapt and change our educational system to match. It is our responsibility to create cultures of innovation that allow us to move beyond the way we've always done it.

If Henry Ford had asked the common man on the street what he wanted in terms of transportation prior to the automobile, it is written that he would have asked for faster horses! Often we know what we know and until leadership inspires a shared vision that challenges the process, often organizations are stymied with "that's the way we've always done it." Unlearning leaders change that! This is the way we do it now! We often do not know what we do not know therefore it's incumbent upon us to become lifelong learners.

UNLEARNING COMMUNITY SERVICE

Every generation of adults has said something along the lines of "Kids these days ..." Those of us who work with children everyday know that students are doing amazing things to add value to their communities and help others. Leyden Community High School District 212 is doing exciting work in order to help students understand the power of service. They want their students to adopt a mindset of service, as opposed to a mindset of "serve-us." Leyden knows that students who give of their time and talents not only can transform their community but can also have a generational impact on themselves, their friends and family, and those around them.

Leyden has identified research-based factors that lead to student success. Those include school attendance, citizenship, career pathways, course completion, and more. That list, along with completion of community service, allows Leyden students to earn the Excellence Award which is recognized at graduation. Students are able to track their progress toward that award throughout high school.

Nick reminds staff members about one particular expectation every year. Specifically, he tells all coaches and club sponsors that he expects them to cancel at least one practice or meeting to take their students to complete a community service project. This simple expectation serves a variety of purposes:

1. Good things happen for those in need throughout our communities.
2. Students discover how it makes you feel to help others.
3. The community learns that "kids these days" care about helping others.

Leyden participates in the annual Make a Difference Day where over 500 of their students spread out throughout the communities to complete a variety of projects alongside their teachers, sponsors, coaches, and administrators. Several years ago, the district created a position titled Director of School and Community Outreach. This individual is specifically responsible for identifying community needs for volunteers and matching student groups to where they can be most helpful. Deerfield's young students take great pride in the variety of philanthropy, service, and community engagement activities as well.

In 2016, Nick made a recommendation to the school board at Leyden that was unusual. He recounted all of the examples of service in the school and community, but pointed out that the district had the word "global" in its mission statement. Even though the district had global service opportunities for students, the cost to participate in these trips was prohibitive for the vast majority of students in the district, where over 60 percent are classified as low-income.

So the discussion at the board meeting was, if the district believes in the importance of global service, then they should use district resources to help support those opportunities. Recall the information about inspiring a shared vision. Nick reminded the community leaders that part of the shared vision was global service. They challenged the status quo to create a new reality aligned with core-values and the mission of the organization.

Now, the board is funding the majority of the cost for student groups to complete global service in the summer. In 2016, groups traveled to Mexico and Peru to work at orphanages, rural schools, mountain villages, and more. Students, many of whom would not have been able to afford these trips, were able to learn about other cultures and experience the power of making a change in the lives of others throughout the world.

It might be easy for school districts to point to existing community service efforts and simply "check the box" in saying that their students do that. However, if we are truly going to prepare our students for the global world that awaits them, we need to rethink what opportunities we create for our students.

UNLEARNING TECHNOLOGY SUPPORT

In 2012, Leyden was one of the first three school districts in the country to go 1:1 with Google Chromebooks and Google Apps for Education. Regardless of the device or operating system your district selects, one question comes up in every district. Who is going to maintain all of these devices? How will the system deal with scratches, dents, and repairs?

There are a variety of ways to answer that question. A district can increase their number of adult technology staff members in order to fix and support devices as necessary. A district can choose to lease devices so that they can send machines off to the company for repairs. A district can contract with a third-party company to provide necessary support. All of those are viable solutions, but Leyden decided on a different path, the creation of a student technology support class. They were unlearning by challenging the process.

Tech Support Internship (TSI) is a class for high school students that runs at both Leyden High Schools every period of the day. In this course, Leyden students serve as level one tech support for all needs in the district. They repair cracked screens, charging ports, keyboards, and more on their classmates' Chromebooks. They help teachers troubleshoot problems with laptops, speakers, and smart boards. Since the creation of the course, over 90 percent of all support tickets have been opened, handled, and closed without adult involvement from the technology department.

Students in TSI also work on developing the soft skills they will need to be successful in the work force someday. They take turns working at the reception desk where they greet visitors, answer telephones, and create support tickets for their classmates. When a student is repairing a device or responding to a work ticket, they document their efforts with professional writing about their processes and progress. Taking risks, trusting students, enabling others to act; all of those actions require unlearning.

When students are not actively responding to support tickets in the TSI class, they choose individual pathways to follow. Many students earn career credentials from Microsoft, Google, CompTia, and more. Those credentials have helped many students earn high-paying part-time jobs while in high school, full-time jobs after high school, and skills that support their efforts in college. Every student has a unique experience (of their choosing) in TSI. Partnerships with local businesses and organizations help support growth beyond the school walls.

Thousands of educators from across the country have visited Leyden and many school districts have modeled their student-led tech support programs after TSI. One question that is always asked is "Who are the teachers for this course?" At Leyden, the teachers come from the Business department and they all have one thing in common. They are willing to adapt and learn alongside their students. These business education teachers have unlearned old ways of instructing. They are now guides on the side instead of sages on the stage.

Those teachers could have said that they don't know how to teach a Tech Support Class. They could have said "That's not what we do in the Business department." Instead, they choose to take responsible risks, be nimble and adaptive, and learn right alongside their students. They went a step further and created a committee of technology leaders in the community.

That group consists of employees from Microsoft, Google, CDW, and a number of other local companies. They unlearned "that's the way we have always done it"—they clearly challenged the process and created new sustainable pathways for education never before imagined.

The teachers meet throughout the year with this advisory board and discuss what is needed in employees today. Based on feedback from that group, the curriculum and opportunities in TSI continue to change so that the students' skills and credentials meet the needs of the work world today.

CHALLENGE THE PROCESS
(SIDEBAR—MID-CHAPTER FEATURE)

The third exemplary practice is *Challenge the Process*. "To do your best as a leader, you have to seize the initiative to change the way things are" (p. 162). As described in this chapter, the unlearning leader clearly challenges multiple processes to innovate and rethink systems and structures. It is not a rejection of the past to create a new present, it's leadership.

"They are the times when you're expected to ask, 'Why do we do this?' But don't just ask this when you're new to the job. Make it a routine part of your leadership" (p. 164). Unlearning leaders ask tons of questions to discover why "it" is taking place the way it is. They constantly seek out ways to improve and create. Like the innovation grant process described in chapter 2, leaders who experiment, take risks, and learn are modeling "challenge the process."

These leaders are not seeking change for change's sake. They are seeking new and better ways to do whatever it is their mission demands. They align the organization's practices to and with the organization's core values. Often there is misalignment and the need for adjustments. These adjustments, or challenges to the process, lead to new and often better ways of doing.

Through the innovation grant experiences in Deerfield and the global studies experiences and changes in Leyden, we create conditions that support safe and courageous leadership to thrive and flourish. Failure is celebrated with unlearning leadership. Through challenge, experimentation, risk taking, and "doing," there are bound to be failures and restarts. When a leader views failure as a first attempt in learning, and when all around them know there is safety in failure, true growth takes place.

One of the greatest challenges schools continue to face as they change from teacher centered places to learner centered places is control and where that control rests. As we and our leadership teams have learned, change is difficult and it requires a steady hand and a steady, focused mind. We have both found that sharing control between teachers and students is challenging. With student technical support teams and student choice in programs, real innovation is exemplified. This is an example of successful ceding or sharing of control.

Challenging existing structures so that new and better structures can take their place is the aim and objective of leaders who master this exemplary practice. In terms of building cultures that sustain this type of collaborative approach, look ahead to chapter 5 in the personalized professional learning section. Another great quote from Kouzes and Posner that captures the essence of this exemplary practice is found on page 188:

> Ward Clapham of the Royal Canadian Mounted Police ... you have to be willing to do things that have never been done before. Every single personal best story ... speaks to the need to take risks with bold ideas. Leaders have to take it a step further ... get others to join them on these adventures of uncertainty. **The difference between exemplary leader & individual risk-taker is that leaders are able to create the conditions where people *want* to join with them in the struggle. Leaders make risk safe ...**

UNLEARNING STUDENT VOICE AND CHOICE

The students' voices should be heard loudly and clearly in an effort to create and sustain the most socially just classrooms. The students' voices and imprint, and cultural experiences should scream loudly enough at curriculum designers and teachers so that higher levels of satisfaction can be realized for students across the country and the world on all levels of the educational spectrum. As Herbert Kohl states in *The New Teacher Book*, "Don't turn teaching for social justice into a grim responsibility, but take if for the moral and social necessity that it is" (44).

TSI is just one example of student voice and choice at Leyden. There has been a national trend to narrow the focus of schools due to high-stakes testing, No Child Left Behind, and other factors. Leyden prides itself on the fact, that through the ebb and flow of national trends, their high schools have remained comprehensive in providing a wide variety of options for college, career, and life readiness.

Located outside of Chicago, Illinois, the Leyden community boasts a significant number of large and small manufacturing companies. Nick believes there is a symbiotic relationship between the schools and the business community. When the businesses flourish, the tax base is strong, and the schools have the resources to provide opportunities for students. To do their part, schools should mirror the local needs so that students, if they choose, have the skills to fill the needs of the local workforce.

With this in mind, Leyden has two of the premier advanced manufacturing classroom labs in the country. With the partnership of local businesses, students learn on Computerized Numerical Control (CNC) machinery that is similar or identical to the equipment located in local businesses. Many of those businesses will hire Leyden students and/or help pay for them to earn advanced degrees. Either way, the students have the choice to access opportunities that exist in their own community.

Similarly, Leyden offers impressive career pathways in the culinary arts and hotel and restaurant management. This is important due to Leyden's proximity to Chicago's O'Hare International Airport. With the airport comes hotels, restaurants, and many jobs. Nick recounts one example where students were given choice in their education and a unique leadership opportunity:

Every year, Leyden hosts an area Board dinner where they welcome school board members and superintendents from the nearby school districts. In 2016, he asked the advanced catering capstone course if they would like to provide the meal for the event. The teacher of the course selected two students to be in charge of the event. Those students researched recipes and built three separate menus complete with salads, main courses, side dishes, desserts, and drinks.

They contacted Dr. Polyak's office and set up a time for a taste testing. The students prepared and plated all three meals for a small number of staff members. They served each meal and explained what they had prepared and why they felt the components complemented one another. Following the tasting, they led a conversation with the staff members as a meal was selected.

One the night of the dinner, those two students became the managers of the event. They supervised their classmates and made sure that the event ran smoothly. Following the dinner, they were thanked by everyone in attendance and answered questions about the process they followed from start to finish.

Why do we share this story? The secret is in the behavior of the teacher, Valerie Berger. As many would expect, she could have easily selected the meal, overseen the preparation and service, and taken a bow following the meal. She did not do that. Instead, she allowed the students an opportunity to take a leadership role and see the event through from start to finish.

Her only participation was to purchase the ingredients necessary for the event. Those two students might follow a path to a career in the culinary arts, or they may not. Either way, however, they took a large step forward in terms of confidence and leadership. Those lessons will serve them well no matter what path they choose. And this all happened simply because a teacher gave them voice and choice in their education.

Another story comes from a pre-engineering classroom at Leyden:

A freshman student had completed all of the assigned work in the course with several weeks remaining in the school year. He asked his teacher a simple question, "What should I do now?"

A teacher in that situation might respond with, "Help some of your classmates with their projects," "Put your head down and be quiet," or the ever-popular "Fill out this worksheet." This particular teacher went another direction when he responded to that question with a question of his own. He looked at that freshman and said, "What would you like to do?"

The student responded that he wanted to create a 3D printed model of his high school. The teacher said "OK" and he got to work. Using Google Earth, a tape measure, a GoPro camera, and AutoDesk Inventor, he programmed one of the school's 3D printers to create a model of the school. When it was complete, he gave the model to his principal as a gift.

The school year was still not over, so the student repeated his process and produced a model of the other high school in the district. That time he completed the model in one third of the time and gave it as a gift to that school's principal.

As the school year was coming to a close, Nick and Mike received an opportunity to attend a MakerSpace event at the White House. Nick approached this student and asked him to repeat this process and create a model of the White House. The student created a 4 by 8 inch model and wrote a letter to President Obama explaining the process and technology he used to create the mini-White House.

The following week, Nick brought the student's model and letter to Washington DC and presented it to the Deputy Director of Technology and Innovation as a gift to be given to the President. Through social media, the student was able to view pictures and video of his creation being delivered.

Why is this story significant? One teacher, Frank Holthouse, took advantage of an opportunity to give a student voice and choice in his education. The student followed his own passion for engineering and 3D printing and was able to not only create gifts for two principals but also a gift for the President of the United States.

Similar stories can be told about students being given 20 percent time in their classes to follow passion projects. Those opportunities have resulted in student created flying drones, video games, and much more. Currently, teachers at Leyden are developing a problem-based learning "school within a school" that will introduce students to authentic, interdisciplinary learning as an option during their freshmen year.

With student leadership in almost every aspect of the schools, the Leyden School Board has taken the logical next step by adding student members to the school board. Those students sit at the board table and participate in discussions and decision-making. This is an example of unlearning governance. This represents respect for student voice and agency at the highest levels.

If school districts are truly to unlearn the idea that our schools are centered around the adults, we need to lead the way in making sure we value our students and involve them in every aspect of the district. School leaders need to foster that culture of innovation and forward thinking so that the other adults in the district feel safe to unlearn what they've always known.

In Deerfield, student voice impacted the design and construction of twelve award winning middle school science labs. The 140 member Superintendent's Task Force for Middle Level Education included student members as well as teachers, parents, community members, administrators, and board members. The decision-making process, the evening meetings, and board presentations all featured students at the table in substantive roles. This was strategic thinking and community engagement unlearned.

Since that Task Force concluded, students have been piloting various device designs and giving input to the teacher Technology Committee. Students have made multiple presentations to the Board of Education on technology, curriculum, options, etc. Student voice also impacted the Deerfield renovation of art and music learning spaces to best meet the needs of modern students. The 1960s era learning spaces no longer made sense. Students are the number one stakeholders, whether five or fifteen years old, their voices count.

In addition to unlearning student voice, the unlearning leader has to unlearn his or her own "classroom." While we commented on the connected educator in chapter 1, in the next chapter we will be highlighting leadership lessons from #suptchat, the Twitter chat we co-moderate. Through this professional learning opportunity, topics have addressed systemic changes and unifying focus points for leaders to unlearn and help their colleagues lead in order to create new structures and systems for second order change and lasting systems growth.

We experienced a new classroom for ourselves in January 2016 when we went on a mission trip to the Dominican Republic to literally help build a new school. The team of volunteers consisted of superintendents, principals, educators, PTA members, and others who all share a passion for serving children and families.

This memory mission trip was sponsored by LifeTouch and supported by the American Association of School Administrators (AASA), the National Association of Elementary School Principals (NAESP), the National Association of Secondary School Principals (NASSP), the National School Boards Association (NSBA), and the National Parent Teacher Association (PTA).

For most parents and kids, crossing the street to catch the school bus may be the riskiest part about getting to school. Can you imagine sending your child on a two and a half mile hike up a mountain in order to receive an education? Or, what if you didn't have the ability to send them to a school at all?

Children in Rio Grande, Dominican Republic face these unfavorable conditions daily. Many choose not to take the long journey to school and stay home instead. With the lack of educational resources in this part of the world, children are being deprived of reaching their full potential.

The memory mission allowed the volunteers to connect back home via a Live on Air Google HangOut. We are grateful to the students and their teachers who made the memory mission trip come alive and relate to their learning in school. Some cool extras related to the Google HangOut included the engagement of several children from the area. By appearing live in our schools and classrooms from the jobsite in the Dominican Republic, we were literally modeling the way for our students and staff back home.

While we were building walls of the school we were breaking down walls of language and culture. While we were building walls with physical force and skill, we were tearing down walls and barriers of emotion and relationships. We unlearned who the experts were. The patience, trust, and cooperation shown by the local Dominican workers turned us all into "expert" school builders.

After this trip and due to the teaching of some very patient workers and supervisors, we now know how to make concrete. We now know how to apply math in real life situations. We might have intellectually known that water, cement, rocks, and sand combine to form concrete, but we never had the opportunity to mix, make, and use concrete with just shovels and buckets until this trip.

We had to engage in authentic learning on this trip. The local workers had to guide us, a help us, and redirect us as needed. We learned cultural and construction lessons. We were faced with real problems every day and we had to solve them. We were faced with real decisions every day and we had to use teamwork every step of the way. We developed friendships, care, concern, and trust and respect for one another each and every day. All of the 4C's (Communication, Collaboration, Creativity, and Critical Thinking) were part of each lesson throughout each day.

When our group first arrived in the Dominican Republic, the community members in Rio Grande were skeptical of our intentions and kept their distance from all of us. Day by day, people saw us come back and build wall after wall for their school. One the third day, we took turns swinging a pick-axe for hours to dig a trench. Covered in sweat, Nick looked up from the digging to find a local man reaching out to take the axe. He then stepped in and took a turn breaking the rocks and digging the trench that would eventually become the sidewalk at the school.

That day we learned the lesson of modeling the way in order to inspire action from others. That local man did not follow our lead on day one. It wasn't until he trusted us and knew that we were invested in his community that he came forward and joined the work. That was one of so many lessons we learned on the trip. We also learned during our home visits, community walks, play and recreation time, and photography experiences. We really learned from the minute we landed to the minute we took off for home.

This was truly a memory mission. Our international crew from the United States, Canada, Brazil, and the Dominican Republic made a huge impact on the lives of the people we set out to serve in Rio Grande. We also did the same for every one of us as well as all of the people with whom we interacted along the way. We were not tourists we were members of the community! We unlearned what a classroom was and could be.

SUMMARY

As a recap we shared a number of case study examples of unlearning the status quo. The hope is that others can replicate these organizational change practices in support of innovative programming and pathways. Often those most in need of voice are overlooked, in this chapter you read how powerful student and stakeholder voice is and how the unlearning leader needs to include others.

In chapter 4, there is an extension of the connected educator messages found in chapter 1 through the leadership lessons of #suptchat. One of the end-of-chapter features, SUPT-chat, originated with the conceptual learning offered through the actual chat on Twitter. Whether you're a Twitter expert or you know nothing about it, after reading chapter 4 we expect to see you at the next #suptchat.

S—Stop and spend time with your leadership team to review the way things are done in your district. Identify the long standing practices that might not be meeting the current needs of your students.

U—Understand what is reasonable to be able to change and when. You are likely to be met with some degree of opposition to suggestion changes. After all, those changes are now how things have always been done. You need to understand what can reasonably be accomplished and what pre-work is necessary before change is possible.

P—Plan for easy ways to allow student voice and choice to enter into their education. Finding small ways to allow students to find their own passions in education will lead to increased capacity in both your students and your staff.

T—Think about how to recognize and encourage a culture of innovation in your schools. When staff knows they have the freedom and support to innovate and students know they get voice and choice in their education, exciting things can happen.

Chat: Pick an edchat, like #urbanedchat: This Twitter chat takes place on Thursday nights starting at 7:00 pm CDT. This is a chat for all urban education stakeholders! http://fuelgreatminds.com/about/urbanedchat/@ UrbanEdChat@theignitedteach.

PRACTITIONER COMMENTARY—SHANE HOTCHKISS

Dr. Shane Hotchkiss is the superintendent of the 1,991 student Bermudian Springs School District in York Springs, Pennsylvania.

I ask a lot of questions. As a new superintendent in December 2011, I began to ask many questions to those around me. I am a person that greatly respects tradition and understands the importance of history. It didn't take long for me to hear a common response to my questions. "Well, we do (this or that) because that's what we've always done." To be honest, I respected that response for a while.

However it became quite clear that many things we were doing were being done just because we've always done it that way. This was regardless of how inefficient the practice, how ineffective the procedure, or how it just lacked common sense. It took a few years, but I was persistent about our need to improve as an organization, make subtle changes, all the while utilizing the resources and expertise we had at our disposal.

It was hard and still is hard, but I could no longer accept the old rationale for doing things. Our organization at Bermudian Springs is amazing. I am not saying that the things we have done in the past were not well done. However, our organization and its needs have changed and we must adapt and not only meet the needs of our current students but also provide an infrastructure that will meet the needs of our future students.

Our school board is very supportive of our vision and makes thoughtful decisions in the best interest of our students and staff. Our administrative team is a solid group of leaders that believes in what we are doing and does an exceptional job of relating to others. Our teaching staff is just as impressive and quite unique. We have a fine blend of experienced teachers along with those new to the profession.

What makes our staff unique is that there are many teachers on our staff that went through our school system as students and are now teaching in the district. Finally, our student population is superb! We really have the greatest kids who work hard, desire to learn, and love our sense of community.

Fast forward a few years to the spring of 2015. I had been the superintendent for almost four years leading an organization that I love and was so supportive. However, I felt that I was in a rut. Our student performance as a district was solid, we have very few behavior issues, and our staff genuinely loves our students and will do whatever they can to support them.

But ... I just didn't feel like we had a K–12 system that was adequately preparing our students for life beyond Bermudian Springs. To be honest, I kept this thought to myself for many months. However, internally I just got to a stage that I could no longer remain silent.

During a school board work session in February 2015, I provided the board with a summary of where I saw our district. I then went on to explain that I would like to convene a committee of teachers, parents, and administrators to discuss the future of teaching and learning within our school district. I wanted the support of our board before I opened Pandora's box.

You see, we are a rural district that is quite conservative and as I previously shared, change is tough. After my discussion with the board there was silence with everyone looking at one another. To break the silence, I used a line that one of my superintendent colleagues (whom I greatly respect) shared with me.

I simply told the board that "I could lawn chair it" or we could begin to have some deep conversations about our students' future. I had to explain that "lawn chairing it" meant that we could all sit back with our feet up and continue to do the things that we've always done. That's easy. That's accepted. But, that's not fair to our students. Fortunately, the board gave their blessing to begin the conversation. I was pumped! Now it was time to unleash a new me—"the lead learner."

The "Future of Teaching & Learning Committee" of twenty individuals met in March 2015. I knew that the things that I thought we should be discussing were going to be difficult for this group as it would take us all out of our comfort zone. I led an ice-breaker activity that was designed to allow all of us to get to know one another on a different level first.

I felt that this was an important process if I was going to get the group to share approaches to teaching and learning that we've never discussed. In a nutshell, the committee was wildly successful and we discussed some pretty far out ideas. Over the coming months we were able to tease out our big ideas and develop a founding for the future of teaching and learning in our district. The framework was shared with our board who continually gave their support to continue the conversation.

We are proud to announce the launch of our One to World Initiative, a program designed to provide our teachers and students with increased access to technology resources in support of their learning in school and at home. This is an exciting opportunity for our teachers and students, and the result of several years of planning, preparation, and consideration of how we can best prepare our students for their futures, today.

Our students will eventually be provided a device and access to resources in support of their learning and that ALL students will have equal access to technology in support of education.

We believe that providing teachers and students with increased access to technology in support of learning will help us:

1. Prepare students with twenty-first-century skills they need to succeed in college or a career.
2. Transform classrooms so that ALL teachers have a classroom resource that supports individualized instruction and engages students in learning.
3. Empower all learners and educators by giving ALL students equal access to information and resources in support of their education.

In order for our initiative to be successful, a tremendous amount of professional development must take place before students receive their new tools. I also believe that as the superintendent I needed to become a learner right alongside our teachers and students. I believe that to have success you must take calculated risks and that means you are going to be uncomfortable at times.

I can honestly say that one of the greatest risks I've taken was as a result of the authors of this book. In February 2015, I took the plunge and joined Twitter. I had spent some time with Mike Lubelfeld and Nick Polyak who were constantly on Twitter. I played along like I knew what it was and how it worked. However, I was clueless.

I found myself watching those two and many others at the National Conference on Education in San Diego use Twitter to connect, communicate, and learn. I was nervous, but began to see the benefits it could bring to me as a learner and as a leader. It was one of the greatest professional learning commitments I've ever made. Twitter is now my go to tool to grow professionally and learn from others while sharing many of the great things we are doing as a district.

This was quite new for our community and district, but I viewed it as a tool with enormous potential for us. I began sharing things on Twitter and talking about it in our schools. I soon noticed a few teachers and administrators joining and connecting with others. I am now very proud to share that more than 60 percent of our staff now have active accounts within the past 12 months.

One of our buildings even used Twitter to lead an entire professional development session for their building. This was definitely not "how we've always done things." "Traditionally" our professional development offerings have been more sit and learn in nature and quite often our administrative team would be on the periphery of the training "looking in."

That's just the way it was always done. As our One to World initiative has progressed through the early stages, I clearly saw the value and importance of our administrators (and myself) working "with" our staff. A prime example of our fresh approach recently occurred during our Google Bootcamp training. A link was sent to all staff members and administrators to sign up. I made sure that I was near the top of the registration list. Within hours of our registration opening we filled two complete sessions of thirty.

I thoroughly enjoyed learning along with the rest of our staff. I wasn't afraid to ask questions and show them that yes in fact an administrator doesn't believe they know all of the answers. I learned from them and I believe I was able to share some things for the good of the order as well. I am thrilled to share that I passed the Google Level I exam! It is my hope that this small snapshot in time becomes the new norm at Bermudian Springs. We are well on our way.

Chapter Four

Unlearning Fear of Social Media

Leadership Lessons from #suptchat

Promise me you'll always remember: You're braver than you believe, and stronger than you seem, and smarter than you think.

—A.A. Milne

Reflection Questions

Can you as a leader learn and grow if you do what you have always done to support your learning?

In what ways are you or should you be engaging in new methods of learning to model the way for your organization?

How are you addressing your worries about not knowing how "the current generation" communicates?

Stop-Think-Act

At the last conference you attended did you meet anyone new? Did you try to seek out new people to meet? Did you follow up with any presenters or participants?

Have you tried one of the Twitter chats referenced in the book? Think about the impact of one hour of free professional learning—give it a try if you have not.

At the next conference you attend, reach out to three other participants. Ask to discuss learning, reflections, and practical applications. Then make a presentation to your leadership team based upon the shared learning. Learn-Reflect-Apply.

WHAT IS #SUPTCHAT

In general, over the past few years, we have found Twitter to be full of relevant, timely, and inspiring professional development. Early in our careers we benefitted from the once a year in-person professional conference, which we do still attend, for our "shot in the arm" of learning and leading. These conferences are also essential for the personal professional relationships and the "humanizing" of technology tools.

Now, with a twenty-first-century reality, we, like our fellow leaders and students, are surrounded by information. How to humanize and increase personal professional relationships and how to stay connected with a group of leaders from around the nation were questions that we sought to answer when #suptchat, the international Twitter chat for superintendents was born.

In October 2014, we created the chat using the a that Minnesota superintendent Daniel Frazier established a few years earlier, #suptchat. This was following the first meeting of the AASA National Superintendent Certification Program in Alexandria, Virginia. The chat was born out of the desire to keep a small group of superintendents connected after an in-person leadership experience. They sought to continue the energy and synergy their group had generated.

The concept of unlearning building relationships from in-person meetings alone gave birth to an effective and far reaching experiment in social connectivity that led to an international twitter chat expanding a professional learning network (PLN) from the East Coast Cohort of a professional organization to the world of superintendents and educational leaders.

What #suptchat has become is a connected forum for leadership with leaders across the world. Connectivity takes many forms, from the traditional to the digital. Leadership lessons from #suptchat permeate the messaging in this book. #suptchat is far more than a chat or an hour a month of free professional learning. #suptchat is representative of new leadership, modern communication, and possibilities. We talk a lot about "twenty-first-century" learning. In actuality, it's 2017 and it is time to look farther down the road for growth, innovation, and success.

The responses and support for new learning, growing, and connecting via the #suptchat forum on Twitter have been affirming and impressive! Every month, we share out an open letter explaining how anyone can participate in the chat. While many leaders have not yet had the chance to participate, it is never too late to jump in.

In general, a Twitter chat is an opportunity and an invitation to spend an hour with other thought leaders and colleagues. In this case, #suptchat takes place "live" on the first Wednesday of every month at 7:00 pm Central (5:00 pm Pacific, 8:00 pm Eastern). Leaders interested in getting automatic reminders about the chat can sign up using Remind by sending the text message @suptchat to 81010, or by visiting the website at: https://www.remind.com/join/suptchat.

An educational chat is like a one-hour conference call, meeting, or symposium. All that is needed is a Twitter account, an hour of time, and an open mind about digital professional learning. You can follow Nick at @npolyak and you can follow Mike at @mikelubelfeld. Their District hashtags are: #leydenpride (Leyden High School District 212) and #engage109 (Deerfield Public Schools District 109).

Whether someone is already a Twitter user or not, they can search these hashtags to get a sense of how our districts' Twitter use communicates and shows the districts' stories as well as the real time learning experiences and opportunities for students, staff, and community. Similarly, the voice of educational leadership, digital leadership, and general leadership is amplified by #suptchat.

In chapter 1, the concept of disconnection was addressed as needing to be "unlearned." #suptchat is a powerful example of how so many have unlearned disconnection and how they actively connect and engage, virtually, to get an hour of professional development every month.

The concepts in chapter 2 about unlearning being stuck in the planning phase also speak loudly to the #suptchat experience. Why join #suptchat? A response could be to experience a Twitter chat yourself. What could you do as a result of #suptchat? Perhaps you will create a chat in your own district. It also enhances and creates relationships. #suptchat continues to connect leaders from around the United States and the world.

The concepts addressed in chapter 3 focused on doing things differently. The #suptchat learning lessons reflect new learning, new communication, new resource curation, and new growth. The leadership lessons of #suptchat continue to evolve. The chat itself is evolving too, for example, at a summer 2016 chat we used a live video tool in addition to Twitter which allowed for live, verbal/video chatting as well.

Unlearning the concept that technology is impersonal resonates with #suptchat participants. When you read a Tweet from a person and then you see the person live, there is a human connection.

The topics that have been addressed in #suptchat are varied and reflect the multitude of complex challenges leaders face every day in all settings across the country (and world). The following is a listing of topics discussed since the chat started in October 2014 through April 2017:

- Inaugural Chat—Connected Leadership
- Future Ready/1:1 Transition
- Communication and Community Engagement
- Project Lead
- Member Submitted Topics on Leadership and the Superintendency
- John Maxwell Leadership Quotes
- #leadexcellence—with AASA president Dave Schuler
- Professional Development and Learning
- Superintendent's Role in Innovation
- Maker Space Movement with Laura Fleming
- John Hattie's 8 Mindframes
- 4 Cs with Edleader 21's CLO
- Branding and Communication with Joe Sanfelippo and Tony Sinanis
- Advice for Aspiring Superintendents
- Personalized Learning
- Most Likely to Succeed (Film and Book) with Ted Dintersmith
- Service and Servant Leadership
- Redefining Ready Initiative
- Future Ready—Collaborative Leadership with U.S. Office of Ed Tech
- Student Voice
- 7 Habits of Highly Effective People
- Summer Work for the Superintendent
- Superintendent Use of Twitter
- Insure All Children Toolkit
- What's New in Social Media
- Education Reimagined
- Effective Communication Strategies between Board of Education and Superintendent
- Selection of Staff Processes

Archives of all chats are available (https://goo.gl/aX8Bal).

Those who participate in #suptchat hail from all over the United States as well as from all over the world. There are countless others who participate by learning, reading, and sharing, but not by active Tweeting live during the chat.

CONNECTING THROUGH TECHNOLOGY

Considering the age or generation of leaders comes into play when identifying relationships with technology. Depending on who you are, social media is new, the iPad is new, and 1:1 computing in classrooms is new. Sometimes the current generation takes for granted just how "new" or "ubiquitous" "technology" is and has become.

For some perspective, and context, some remember Netscape Navigator, the web browser from 1995. That was revolutionary in 1995. Google was born in 1997, the iPod was born in 2001, Facebook in 2004, Twitter in 2005, the Amazon Kindle in 2007, and the iPhone in 2008. In the 2017–2018 school year, the students entering kindergarten were born in 2011 or 2012.

Those children will never have known a world without the iPad, iPod, touch screens, Google, etc. The children of today do not ever have to deal with busy signals on phones or television channels with the colorful bars that signified an end to programming. For additional perspective let's look at television. The television was first introduced in 1939, then 23 years later color TV was introduced (in 1962). It was not until 1993 when HD (high definition) was introduced. And now, in 2017 television itself is more of a concept than a thing. TV can be watched on smart phones, tablets, anywhere and anytime.

The leadership lessons from #suptchat tell the story of a world where leaders do not enjoy the freedom to use technology or not. The leaders of this world, in public education, industry, government, etc., are tasked with preparing the leaders of the future. It is incumbent upon them, therefore, to get with the times and lead as the people expect them to lead, not as they did in the past.

Social media usage is not an option, it's an expectation. Just as Wi-Fi connectivity is this generation's electricity, so too is social media this generation's soda shop. Leaders must go where the people are. That is changing rapidly with the advancement and acceleration of technological tools.

When considering Kouzes and Posner's Five Exemplary Practices (Model the Way, Inspire a Shared Vision, Challenge the Process, Enable Others to Act, and Encourage the Heart) the use of technology as a tool for connections proves relevant in each. For example, when the leader wants members of the organization to use technology tools the leader must model the way.

Through modeling, the "why" is defined, shared, and identified. This "why" helps Inspire a Shared Vision. The entire book is really about challenging commonly held beliefs and actions, the processes and methods of leadership, using the public school system as the main foundation, connecting via technology, and challenging the process of old school connections.

The traditional in-person model of conference professional learning does not immediately lead to connections. But through focusing on leading in a culture of connectivity and becoming a connected educator, even the most isolated conference situation can lead to an opportunity for growth and application of connectivity.

Many conferences involve attending alone, not knowing anyone, or attending with your team, and not meeting anyone new. One way to turn this disconnected experience into an experience designed to breed connectivity can be found by intentionally aiming to make a connection with the hope of forming a lasting relationship.

The superintendent who deliberately seeks out connections and opportunities to network, share, learn, and grow is the one who is leading that way on the home turf too. Seek out what types of conferences teachers or school leaders are planning to attend, and then attend with them. This practical and proactive approach to learn together builds relationships and allows for greater growth for all involved.

In consideration of enabling others to act, #suptchat as an example, has allowed hundreds of leaders to participate in a Twitter chat who otherwise might have had no use for or understanding of the power of Twitter as a connection tool. Enabling others to act through sharing and professional development and live streaming of onsite presentations via applications such as Periscope, or Facebook Live, or any number of other powerful and free technology tools connects people who might not be able to be physically present but who can be engaged from off-site.

Finally, encouraging the heart is realized as a practice when leaders connect with others and recognize the value of colleagues across the country, state, and world. Through recognizing, imitating, studying, learning, and connecting, far more stories of success get noticed and shared. We can all now tell stories and connect with people, because smart phones, social media, and so many other tools have made connecting via technology ubiquitous in most settings.

ENABLE OTHERS TO ACT
(SIDEBAR—MID-CHAPTER FEATURE)

The fourth exemplary practice is *Enable Others to Act*. Hire great people and get out of the way is a saying that many leaders, including presidents, are often associated with. We wrote about selection of staff in chapter 2. We also share many examples of building a positive organizational culture and measuring both climate and culture as a regular part of unlearning. Find out what is going on, share that information, and collaboratively change.

By rejecting "that's the way we have always done it" as written in chapter 3, the unlearning leader must enable others to act in order to create a new and powerful organizational structure. Kouzes and Posner found that this fourth exemplary practice of leadership is inherently tied to the fostering of collaboration by building trust and facilitating relationships.

In the summer 2016 *Journal of Scholarship & Practice*, Mike and two of the principals with whom he serves published a commentary about respect, culture, and essentially creating a culture enabling others to act. From their commentary:

[Bullis, Filippi, and Lubelfeld] support the five strategies of effective communication in action (Establish Individual Relationships, Solicit and Share Feedback From Stakeholders, Engage External Environments, Treat Every Communication As If It Were a First Impression, Celebrate Growth) whereby the stakeholders demonstrate that communication is something with which they are a part; communication is not "done" to them it is done with them. (p. 52).

Their five strategies of effective communication lay the groundwork for establishing a culture where capacity is built. Nick's staff exemplifies this with both learner agency and teacher agency. They have engaged teacher creativity to build modern day manufacturing programs and they have recently established student members of the school board, as two examples.

These beliefs in action and structures that enable others to act is a cornerstone of the unlearning leader. Best ideas emanate from collaboration. Defined autonomy is an example of how senior leaders can allow and support all school leaders to become site-based. There are macrolevel goals and objectives that all follow, yet each leader has a unique footprint or fingerprint of their own leadership that needs to be nurtured and supported.

Through creating conditions where change and courage are rewarded, the unlearning leader gets the opportunity to try new leadership methods and apply those which work and discard those that don't. The unlearning leader enables others to act so he does not have to shoulder the entire burden of the leadership process.

#SUPTCHAT ARCHIVES

After each chat, we create an archive of the tweets. What this means is that a digital record of the one-hour conversation is stored and shared so folks who are interested can go back and see what the conversations were about. It also allows anyone at anytime to "rejoin" the conversations and access links, blogs, resources, etc. The topics have been varied as listed earlier in the chapter. The power of the chat exists in the instant, live chat as well as in the archive.

For example, during the May 2015 chat, with the topic of professional development, the questions are given in Table 4.1.

Tweeting participants for that month came from Illinois, Missouri, Minnesota, Iowa, Virginia, Washington, D.C., New Jersey, Texas, Wisconsin, New York, and California, and non-Tweeting visitors may have come from anywhere. The diversity of thought and perspective adds to the richness of the monthly chat. In Figure 4.1, we're sharing some examples or responses to the sixth question about what suggestions people had for book studies and why. With #suptchat the learning is instant, ongoing, and permanent.

Table 4.1   #suptchat Questions from the Inaugural Chat October 2014

Q1: As a school superintendent what makes you come to work each day? #suptchat

Q2: Why is it important for us to network with each other and share throughout the country? #suptchat

Q3: What are the top three issues your district faces? #suptchat

Q4: Why do you think that the Chicago Bears are superior to every other team in the National Football League? #suptchat

Q5: What is the most important data point that you track to measure success in your district? #suptchat

Q6: What strategies have you used to cut costs in your district or to deal with reduced funding streams? #suptchat

Nick will share a poll for topic choice for next chat

Q7: What is the best book, author, publication, etc. ... that all superintendents should be reading and why? #suptchat

Q8: What strategies do you use to encourage/empower student voice within your school district? #suptchat

Q9: What is the role of technology (1:1 or technology in general) in schools? #suptchat

Q10: What strategies do you use to tell your district's story both in and out of your community? #suptchat

In chapter 3, there was a feature on student voice and choice. In May 2016, that was the topic for #suptchat. Participants hailed from British Columbia (Canada), Shenzhen, China, Kentucky, Illinois, Texas, Pennsylvania, Missouri, Wisconsin, California, Virginia, Georgia, Minnesota, Indiana, Connecticut, New York, Kansas, Iowa, and Maryland. The global views on student voice and choice inform all of us as with various, divergent viewpoints.

Another huge benefit of chat participation and learning is the vast resources and idea generation. The whole idea behind unlearning is opening oneself to the possibilities of other realities and other ways of doing "it" better and differently. Seeking out national and international viewpoints in a deliberate and intentional manner allows the unlearning leader to expand opportunities for himself/herself and those in the organization and communities where they serve.

PLNS, TWITTER, VOXER

Among the greatest lessons learned from #suptchat is that there are many more leaders out there craving personal learning community support as evidenced by the hundreds of participants in #suptchat every month, as well as in attendance at state and national conference presentations on this topic.

The PLN (personal or professional learning community) is expanded through finding both like-minded and unlike-minded "people" (experts,

Figure 4.1 Tweets from #suptchat from the Inaugural Chat in October 2014.

Figure 4.1 (continued)

colleagues, friends, authors, speakers, etc.) A phenomenon oft repeated at in-person conferences or workshops is "Oh, I know you from Twitter," "It's great to meet you in person," or "I read your blog." The growth and expansion of the PLN via technology tools like Twitter increases the depth and opportunity for personal professional development and relationships to be formed.

If a school leader truly understands the functionality of connectivity, he/she is more likely to learn with the other teachers and leaders in the organization. If that school leader is not aware, he/she may thwart the efforts of innovative teachers. For example, a friend of Mike's is a teacher and he received great pushback from his principal when he wanted to use Twitter in support of his instruction.

Two years later, under a new administration, that same teacher taught a summer school math class completely online, and via Twitter! So we can only imagine how much growth and opportunity this teacher and his students would have had if his earlier administrator was technology savvy/literate and supportive of a connected culture.

Clearly this teacher is a digital leader. Clearly this teacher is inspiring his students and empowering them to connect with the world of mathematics (his subject area) through their world of communication (i.e., Facebook, Twitter, Google Apps for Education, etc.). School leaders should reach out to their own professional associations as well as local, in-person groups of administrators to move their local organizations forward.

While Twitter may be our main "go to" social media tool for a multitude of reasons, the two-way radio app Voxer has become another "go to" for developing and sustaining a PLN and for varied communications for leaders across the nation. Voxer allows for asynchronous and synchronous communication using voice, text, images, and video.

Voxer groups of up to 500 members can be formed for communications. We belong to a number of national Voxer groups for example we communicate with educational leaders via an innovative iSupt group on Voxer. This group has superintendents, assistant superintendents, and professional association leaders working together to address and identify problems of practice.

We frequently discuss our usage of Voxer to help solve real-life problems of practice. When faced with a unique situation or difficult problem, we often use Voxer to ask our PLN for help. Sometimes colleagues respond right away. Other people might hear the message later in the day and respond. Either way, we are able to tap into the collective expertise of friends from across the country from a simple app on our phones.

The superintendent is no longer a lonely position. Twitter connects. Voxer connects. These social media tools are but two of many new and growing communication tools designed to "flatten the world" in terms of removing barriers and supporting and promoting collegiality and fellowship among leaders. A growing number of districts are using Voxer to connect members of the district leadership team for instant communication and operations at the local level.

Twitter has allowed us to connect in unique and modern ways. One example is from Mike when he was in attendance at a meeting of superintendents where the Governor of Illinois was the keynote speaker. The Governor sent out some tweets about supporting public education. Mike tweeted a "thank you" and included an invitation for the Governor to visit the Deerfield Public Schools. Through Twitter, the Governor accepted the invitation and visited one of his hometown school districts. Without Twitter would Mike have even invited the Governor?

Nick was attempting to impact Illinois legislation to allow for virtual "snow days" to leverage technology to reduce instructional interruptions. He went to Twitter and discovered John Trout, a fellow superintendent in Indiana was already utilizing virtual snow days in his district. Due to Twitter, Nick connected with this leader in Indiana.

They shared resources, ideas, and philosophies about how to deal with snow days in our new technological age. As it turns out Nick's district was one of three Illinois school districts allowed by law to run virtual snow days. Thanks to Twitter, Nick formed a new relationship with a neighboring state superintendent and helped further a local legislative agenda.

Polyak (2016) describes this relationship created as a result of social media in the September issue of School Administrator magazine:

> *Last year, I was working with several colleagues to create legislation that would allow school districts in Illinois to run virtual snow days, something we called E-Learning Days. I turned to Twitter and found John Trout, a superintendent in Elkhart, Ind., who was tweeting about the same topic in his former district. I reached out to him, and he soon became an invaluable resource for me (and really for Illinois) as we implemented a pilot program in our state. More importantly, Trout and I are now part of each other's learning networks.* (9)

This acceptance and embracing of social media is truly a scary concept for many whose entire professional life has involved being trained before implementing anything. For schools to change, for school systems to change, for instruction to change, so must our concept of training. To steal a catchy phrase from Nike, we need to "just do it" and the training takes the form of a hands-on, live learning experience!

These past few years have been explosive in terms of instructional, educational, and operational advances in technology tools. Exciting and energizing are the many uses, connections, learning opportunities, and growth opportunities that many have enjoyed as a result of technology. An elusive and evolving term, technology is becoming more of a concept. In chapter 2, the focus was on unlearning the change process in order to do change and execute plans through action.

In this chapter, the focus has been on leadership lessons from #suptchat. The large, macrolessons are related to the power of connecting with others and learning from others in order to replicate their successes and learn from their failures. Failure is encouraged in change leadership.

The chat continues to address and open up discussion on large and small issues of importance to superintendents and other leaders. The moderators welcome and encourage others to join in. For example, when Laura Fleming co-hosted in July 2015, the chat participants enjoyed getting to know many from Laura's PLN.

Laura is a leading librarian and one of the nation's foremost experts on the Maker Movement. Through the monthly topic of making, #suptchat connected superintendents, teachers, librarians, and others. The power of connection is a major take-away.

We are grateful to the support of the American Association of School Administrators for their involvement and promotion of the chat as an additional means of communication and growth for their international membership of leaders. The chat has focused on leadership initiatives from AASA as well as other organizations like the Office of Educational Technology from the White House and the United States Department of Education.

Leadership lessons from #suptchat include the need to engage with others, listen to others' experiences, share with others and synergize multiple ideas, viewpoints, and perspectives. In chapter 5, we will look at the overall changes in professional learning including microbadging, personalized learning, new formats and structures in large group learning, and partnerships with professional associations.

We recognize that Twitter chats, tools like Voxer, and other current tools and trends, are what works now. The unlearning leader not only embraces those opportunities, but also recognizes that the tools will change in the years ahead. We all need to be flexible so that we are able to adjust as leaders in schools and in a world that will be changing around us.

SUMMARY

As a recap, the leadership lessons of #suptchat allow the reader to unlearn that technology is cold, sterile, or anti-social. On the contrary, the unlearning leader finds greater, stronger, more meaningful relationships as a result of the leverage of technology. The very beginning of the chat itself was born out of a desire to keep an in-person leadership group connected during the separation between group meetings.

#suptchat is successful because it is a virtual place for connected leaders to stop in, make, affirm, and sustain virtual relationships that also can and do exist in person. Imagine the professional and personal affirmation when a familiar face goes from thumbnail image to actual friend. Technology humanizes and enhances relationships. The unlearning leader applies that precept into all areas of leadership.

S—Stop and reflect on the central ideas of this chapter and think about how you will implement one or more of the suggestions. Ask yourself:

- Are you using any technology to connect with others?
- Have you experimented with Twitter? Voxer?
- Do you write a regular column/article in your local newspaper?

U—Understand how your story and your experiences shape the lens with which you view the world and your leadership. Communication is best when it starts with listening. Listen to understand and you'll connect powerfully. Understand how technology is about people not devices. Open your mind to the ideas of others.

P—Plan to try to use new technology tools to connect.

Commit to using Twitter/Voxer, to writing a blog, or to writing an article in the local newspaper. Who in your area can help you make that leap? Deliberately plan to listen without distractions.

T—Think of a key take-away from this chapter. What confused you or called you to action?

Chat: Pick an edchat, like #satchat which takes place every Saturday morning with educators from across the country. For ease in chatting via Twitter, use Tweetdeck, a reference guide is located in Appendix A.

PRACTITIONER COMMENTARY— JARED COTTON

Dr. Jared Cotton is the superintendent of the 7200 Henry County Public Schools in Collinsville, Virginia.

When I was first named the superintendent in Henry County (in southside Virginia), I was eager to engage with the community to take the school division to the next level. Having served as an associate superintendent in Virginia Beach, I utilized Twitter on a periodic basis, but did not use it enough to see the value.

As a new superintendent, I made the decision to set up a new Twitter account and quickly checked with my technology director to see if my Twitter feed could be posted on our website. To my surprise, I learned that Twitter was blocked from our school division website and access to Twitter was blocked at all schools.

This led to a powerful conversation about the use of Twitter and whether it has educational value to a school division. It also led to concern about what might be posted and the fact that a school division cannot control inappropriate content that is posted by others.

We took a risk, and it has made all the difference.

Even today, I have superintendent colleagues ask why I use Twitter or "What's the point?" Many note that they do not have time to keep up with Twitter. I tell them that I used to feel the same way. However, using Twitter and other social media tools has had such a profound impact on my job that I would encourage all superintendents to give it a try!

One of the first lessons I learned about using Twitter as a superintendent is that it creates an opportunity to share all of the positive things that are happening in our school division. I have used it as a tool to remind the community of upcoming events that they may want to attend. As I attend events throughout the school year, I take a quick picture or video and share with the school community.

I find that parents and students quickly respond, retweet, or "like" these posts. Twitter has helped to change the narrative for our school division as people notice the great things that are taking place. This helps get the word out about the great things happening each day in our schools.

As a result of sharing good news on Twitter, I have also found that Twitter is a powerful tool for instilling school and school division pride. We have created a hashtag that we use for many of our posts—#HCPSPride. I use this hashtag frequently when I share good news about our school division. After several months of this, something great happened. Several of our principals asked if they could create Twitter accounts for their schools so that they could share student and teacher accomplishments with their school communities.

Soon after, teachers started to create Twitter accounts. We even scheduled a "Genius Bar" at our annual teacher and learning conference to teach teachers how to setup and use their very own Twitter accounts. As a result, we have close to 100 staff members now sharing good news about their schools, our students, and our school division each week. What a great PR campaign!

Certainly, Twitter is a powerful communication tool for the entire school community. I learned this lesson very quickly when I sent my first Tweet about schools closing due to inclement weather. Almost immediately, every high school student on Twitter followed me! Although I don't share this often, this is a great strategy for increasing the number of followers on Twitter!

While this is an extreme example, I have found that Twitter is a great tool for communicating important information to the public.

Now when we send home a letter to parents about a school incident or safety concern, we also post the information on Twitter and Facebook with a link to related documents or resources. This has created another avenue for timely communication to our stakeholders.

In addition to the communication benefits we now enjoy, I was also surprised to find that Twitter offers a wealth of powerful learning for me as a leader. While my initial purpose for utilizing Twitter was to communicate with our school community more effectively, I found that it had a significant impact on my professional learning and development.

By following key thought leaders in K–12 education today, I have found that my professional reading has increased exponentially. For example, I typically get links to research studies or reports related to areas of interest in my daily Twitter feed. Many times, I forward links to these resources to my personal e-mail so that I can read them later.

At other times, I forward links to members of my staff and building principals. As a result, I feel that I am better informed of educational research, trends, and successful practices in K–12 education. I especially appreciate the ease with which I am able to share my new learning with others.

The final and most important point I want to make is that Twitter has greatly expanded my PLN. As many know, the superintendency can be a lonely job. Through Twitter, I have "met" colleagues in online Twitter chats (#suptchat) and posts over the past several years. These colleagues are from all over the country and it is exciting to meet many of them in person when I attend conferences and special events. When we meet, we have an instant connection.

Most importantly, I feel that I can reach out to my colleagues if I need assistance. I recently connected with a superintendent in California who is working to provide digital resources for students in lieu of traditional textbooks. In Henry County, we are working on the same issue. Connecting with this superintendent has saved our school division countless hours of trial and error.

The comfort of knowing that I have colleagues easily available if I need assistance has been the most important benefit of Twitter for me. More importantly, if it wasn't for Twitter, we would have most likely NEVER met.

As a superintendent, Twitter has been a significant resource for me. While some superintendents are reluctant to create a Twitter account, I would say that it is certainly worth the effort. Several of my staff members had grave concerns about allowing folks to use Twitter across the school division. By far, the positives have outweighed any issues or concerns that have arisen. Come join our strong PLN on Twitter! You won't be disappointed!

Chapter Five

Unlearning Professional Development

Far and away the best prize that life offers is the chance to work hard at work worth doing.

—Theodore Roosevelt

Reflection Questions

When you plan an in-service in your district, do you think about the best and worst inservices you've attended?
Have you participated in an EdCamp-style unconference?
What is the philosophy or foundation of your professional learning?
In what ways are you meaningfully connected to a professional organization?

Stop-Think-Act

Look at your district's professional learning plan for the year.
Do you have staff input in the organization or structure of learning?
Add an EdCamp or choice-based workshop format to next year's menu of professional learning in your district.

PERSONALIZED PROFESSIONAL
LEARNING AND MICROBADGING

When school leaders listen to the voice of the people, they are connected and the likelihood of their success increases. They are deliberate and intentional about turning learning opportunities into connections and networks. In chapters 1 and 4, we spent considerable time describing deliberate ways for leaders to connect and expand their professional learning network. Connecting and networking should also be done at home in your schools and in your district.

Brown, Domenech & Sherman (2016) describe a vision for a personalized twenty-first-century curriculum (56). This is related to the trend toward personalized professional learning in that both curriculum for students and curriculum for staff call for revised processes. Both classroom curriculum that is personalized and professional learning that is personalized need creation, monitoring, and plans to sustain. All of this is enhanced with networks and PLN partners who help support new learning.

That network, or PLN, needs to exist both inside and outside of the organization. When a leader is asking teachers what their learning needs are, following up with learning opportunities reflective of those needs, and communicating through words and actions, the school leader is connecting and leading through professional learning. The leader, in this case, is unlearning old ways of command control and sit and get professional development.

In our experiences and professional practice, we regularly seek input from stakeholders. Leading in a culture of unlearning is all about connecting with others, valuing their input, and being open to innovation. Leaders today need to meet the needs of multiple generations of workers. The differences in generations are considerable. For example, in a typical school the principal will attend to the needs of people born in the 1950s to the 1990s. It's exciting and challenging to integrate and blend the needs and offerings for all.

The traditional in-person model of conference professional development does not immediately lend itself to connections. But through focusing on creating a culture of connectivity, even the most isolated conference situation can lead to opportunities for connections. Many conferences involve attending alone, not knowing anyone, or attending with your team and not meeting anyone new. Even conferences in a particular school district can be isolating and lonely experiences. The unlearning leader knows that this must change.

As research about student learning shows, students learn and grow more when they have voice and choice in their learning. Adult learners also learn and grow more when they have the same opportunity to provide a voice in their learning. People like to be acknowledged and rewarded for learning. Adults also like to have their views and beliefs affirmed.

One of the more modern approaches to professional development involves microbadging or microcredentialing. Microbadging attends to multigenerational needs and multiple interests and abilities of the learners. We will look at how this model is being used in Deerfield a little later in this chapter.

When employees feel respected and valued they have a greater likelihood of following through with the district/school initiatives. This helps to Inspire a Shared Vision (the I in MICEE). When the leader of the organization connects with the beliefs and feelings and desires of the members of the organization, there is greater support for changes and initiatives as well.

There are several ways to apply unlearning concepts through professional learning to impact organizational culture. Unlearning starts during the transition to a new job, in the first days, and if done correctly, it never stops. Schools have been addressing differentiated needs of students for many years, the unlearning leader also addresses the differentiated needs of the adults.

The leader can demonstrate connectivity and awareness in terms of acknowledging and meeting their needs. When a leader puts forth professional development opportunities that the teachers request or identify as high value, the leader is demonstrating the power of connection and valuing their opinions. By offering options and providing choice, the professional development has a greater likelihood of becoming job-embedded and impactful.

A skilled and connected leadership team meets needs of employees and provides staff learning and development that is in tune with the needs of the teachers. While many leaders celebrate the value of differentiated instruction for student learning, a connected leader, as mentioned, seeks out that which differentiates staff learning and deploys that staff development at varying levels and formats.

In addition, the leader who is physically present at in-service events and workshops and learns alongside the other educators is shaping the culture whether they realize it or not. Personalized professional learning can also refer to personal time with the learners. Often, leaders are reminded of the "need for training" as an expectation or a barrier toward implementation and acceptance of new educational and instructional opportunities.

One way to convince teachers of this and help those who are nervous or reluctant is to actually sit and work with them. As an example, Mike has helped teachers set up their Google calendars in an effort to support the change and to learn and teach together. Leaders can provide one-on-one coaching as effectively as leading whole and small group workshops.

Training in general needs to match the needs of the stakeholders, just like students should be in classrooms where their individual needs are met. The school leader must champion a professional environment where the individual needs of teachers must also be met. To change the concept of training requires courage, support, assistance, and collaboration. Asking teachers to help lead courses, workshops, etc., is an actionable first step in the quest for a redesigned professional development concept.

When Mike came to Deerfield, Jeff Zoul also started as the Assistant Superintendent for Teaching & Learning. Zoul and his team recommended a revamping of the district's professional learning structures. With input from focus groups of teachers, survey data, and a knowledge of best practices, the district embarked on an improvement journey.

The Teaching & Learning departments at both of our districts have created progressive and teacher-focused, student-centered professional learning programs. Dr. Zoul created both the Deerfield College and the Deerfield University professional learning platforms. In addition to those voluntary after school, in-person professional learning programs, Deerfield also partnered with neighboring and nearby districts to offer administrative and teacher learning locally with regional leaders like Garnet Hillman as well nationally with leaders like Tom Guskey, Todd Whitaker, and Rick Wormeli to name a few.

After meeting with teachers across all campuses in Deerfield, it became clear that the organization needed a shot in the arm with respect to professional learning. The staff had not organized as an entire unit in many years, and few could remember any staff input into professional development or staff development options. The new leadership team was very interested in changing both perceptions of and impact of learning for the adults!

After the first staff institute day, and after survey data and focus group interview data was reviewed and analyzed by leadership team members, new offerings were immediately in the works. First, it was clear that many staff members had varying needs and interests, which is probably true in every organization. Many staff members wanted to share input, expertise, and views.

In addition to the formal institute days and inservices, there was some experimentation and innovation brewing in the leadership team. A voluntary, after school professional learning option was born. It was called "Deerfield College." Weekly, once or twice a week for 90 minutes, staff members would teach courses of interest to their peers. Inspiring a shared vision of excellence around teachers teaching teachers really took off.

After the first year of the voluntary Deerfield College, there were:

- 40 Deerfield College classes total
- 668 attendees at these 40 classes
- The 668 total attendees included 238 different staff members from across the district reflecting more than 50 percent of all employees

- 31 staff taught or co-taught a Deerfield College class
- 1 Deerfield College class was filmed and is available here: http://vimeo.com/91366716.

Following the success of the Deerfield College, Zoul, Marcie Faust, Director for Innovative Learning, and their team created the Deerfield University. This program offers an online, voluntary, anytime personal professional learning environment across six virtual campuses: connected learning, grading, reporting and assessment, home/school connection, lesson and unit design, and project-based learning.

There is also the option to create individual pathways. Each campus contains virtual courses, with forty-three total courses currently available. Each course features a learn, do, reflect format. The teachers choose to attend the course, complete the work, and learn and grow.

This voluntary, personalized, professional learning program is showing that people are participating for the intrinsic reward of learning and progressing through the coursework rather than doing the work specifically for any material prize. The Deerfield University program has generated interest externally as leaders across the country are looking for new ways to engage staff in "just in time" learning.

The unlearning leader does not wait for the annual institute day to offer learning, she/he offers learning 24/7 as the current society demands. The unlearning leader selects and hires the best and steps out of the way to support powerful ideas from the team.

HOSTING SYMPOSIA AND SITE VISITS

For many people, and for many years, professional development has meant attending a workshop offsite, taking a class offsite, or bringing in a high priced keynote speaker for a sit and get assembly on site. We have, on many occasions, seen educators judge professional development activities based on whether or not they were entertained and whether or not the session finished early. Unfortunately, it is rare to find canned professional development that meets the learners exactly where they are or provides relevancy in their world.

When Leyden was preparing for their digital conversion in 2012, a group of representatives traveled to Mooresville Graded School District in North Carolina to learn about successfully transitioning to a 1:1 learning environment. They brought the school board president, the teachers' union president, teachers, administrators, and technology staff. In this model of professional development, educators wanting to make a change were able to learn from other educators who had already made a similar change. The "experts" at

Mooresville were able to tell Leyden what worked, and perhaps more importantly, what didn't work.

When the team from Leyden returned to Illinois, they did so with the confidence to move forward with their initiative while also expanding their PLN to a community of friends in North Carolina who could answer questions and help throughout the process. This is a new model of professional development, where practitioners are the experts, and where together we help each other get better. In today's world of social media and connectivity, colleagues and friends are accessible and available at all times. The PLN knows no time or space boundaries.

After receiving that help from Mooresville and others, Leyden made the decision to adopt a "pay-it-forward" mindset. For the past 5 years, they have been hosting annual single-day site visits as well as a very popular multiple-day summer symposium. The staff at Leyden shares their story and advice to school leaders from across Illinois the United States, and beyond.

Thousands of educators have visited Leyden and the learning doesn't stop when people leave. The relationships remain so that participants continue to reach out for help and advice. In return, Leyden learns from all of those school districts and finds ways to improve as well. Through this sharing and communicating, new ways of practicing public education emerge.

School leaders should be present and participate in training and development alongside teachers and others so that they may lead and learn via the lenses of those with whom they seek to impact. This keeps the leaders in tune with what is going on in the system, and it keeps relationship building at the forefront in all encounters.

The key is unlearning the thought that good ideas only exist in classes, workshops, keynotes, or from highly-paid speakers. Some of the most meaningful professional development can come from educators sharing with educators, as long as leaders are willing to take the time to share and support one another. Unlearn the concept that you cannot be a prophet in your own land and break that barrier. We are all better together.

ENCOURAGE THE HEART
(SIDEBAR—MID-CHAPTER FEATURE)

This fifth exemplary practice of leadership, *Encourage the Heart*, is impactful enough to warrant a separate book of the same title! Whether it is one-on-one private recognition, a handwritten note, a group recognition, or a community wide celebration, taking time to personalize, humanize, and emotionally connect is part of this practice. Leaders who connect with people on a positive, authentic, meaningful, and regular way are more admired.

When is the last time you were given meaningful feedback from a superior? When is the last time you gave meaningful feedback to someone else? Kouzes and Posner share that "Motivation to perform a task increases only when employees have a challenging goal and receive feedback on their progress" (282). Do you know the names of your co-workers' spouses or children? Think about how you can encourage the heart today.

Encouraging the heart comes in many shapes and forms. It could be a redesign of classroom learning spaces with staff input. It could be an award ceremony. It could be public or private. It could be personal or in a group. The point is that people's hearts need to be acknowledged and recognized. As referenced in this chapter, encouraging the heart is also present in asking teachers to be presenters.

It is incredibly important to remember that we are all in the "people business" and people are both emotional and rational. It is written that before a child can learn one must make a relationship with him/her (emotional connection). The same holds true for adults. Adults will choose to be far more productive and loyal to a leader they like, respect, and feel likes and respects them.

When we do employee survey work, recognition is often the most neglected dimension by managers. For recognition to be appreciated, it must be timely and perceived as an earnest expression from a caring colleague. Get to know your coworkers as human beings and understand how they prefer to be acknowledged, recognized, and rewarded. Then catch them doing things right and give them praise with enthusiasm.

A famous quote credited to Drucker is that "Culture eats strategy for breakfast." This embodies the point that relationships, culture, and how people feel supersedes strategic or impersonal actions of leadership. From Kouzes and Posner: "Recognition should be personalized; otherwise it will quickly be forgotten and discounted" (285). Unlearning leaders know that relationships are far more valuable than anything, so they recognize their staff. They encourage the heart and support and nurture the human side of education.

PARTNERSHIPS WITH PROFESSIONAL ASSOCIATIONS

We try to make a habit of sharpening everyone else's saws. This section takes a closer look at how we sharpen our own saws. Enjoying exciting and unique professional experiences as a result of years of professional partnerships, we have been to the White House, the Dominican Republic, in the nation's top school districts, and we have been at the forefront of innovative leadership programs.

We have learned how to unlearn and create innovative districts and leadership systems through membership and partnership in and with professional associations. In fact, we first met at an Illinois School of Advanced Leadership (ISAL) program sponsored by the Illinois Association of School Administrators (IASA). We learned that membership was one level of growth and access but partnership opened up a whole new series of leadership opportunities.

We have partnered with our state and national organizations to improve our impact and legacy as leaders. Through unlearning old ways and through innovative partnerships, our experiences have taken us across our home state as well as across the United States. Our partnership even took us overseas on a mission trip. As mentioned in chapter 4, the entire #suptchat story is based on our desire to keep a national leadership group connected between leadership learning sessions.

Our partnerships have allowed us to be part of the changing of the guard of superintendents around the nation. There is a leadership change afoot and a future focus is taking hold across the nation and world. We have experimented with various opportunities and learned from the best of the best in order to improve our impact at home.

We had the opportunity to attend an event at the White House and the United States Patent and Trademark Office in 2015 focused on the Maker Movement in education. While there, we recognized several superintendents at the next table as people took we knew from Twitter. We walked over and introduced ourselves to them in person.

Those chance meetings took relationships that started on social media and made them into real connections. Through reaching out to others at that meeting, we were able to further develop our own PLNs. This is another example of how technology can actually humanize personal relationships.

AASA posted the following commentary after that event at the White House:

"The Maker Movement is about innovation," said Nick Polyak, superintendent of Leyden High School District 212 in Franklin Park, Ill. "It's about the future of our country and the future of our world. We need creators. We need inventors."

"If we're not helping to create that in public education, than who else will," added Polyak, co-moderator of #suptchat, a monthly Twitter chat that engages superintendents about critical issues in public school leadership on the first Wednesday of each month.

"This is a career-high moment for me," said Mike Lubelfeld, superintendent of Deerfield Public School District 109 in Deerfield, Ill. "This is part of the new transformation of education. It's the path to personalization and hopefully the path away from the focus on accountability and standards to a focus on accountability for performance and making."

Retrieved from: http://www.aasa.org/headlinecontent.aspx?id=37484.

Meetings and relationship building, like that anecdote from the White House Makers event, have been repeated over and over throughout the country at professional gatherings and deliberate meetings. Other examples of transforming relationships from virtual to personal have taken place in other partnerships.

We are advisory board members of the AASA Digital Consortium. With meetings and workshops joining leaders from all parts of the United States and Canada, Twitter profile pictures are replaced with in-person relationships formed in pursuit of common goals.

From the AASA Digital Consortium visits, thought leadership sessions, design thinking activities, and prototyping experiences to the National Superintendent Certification program, our PLN expanded far beyond the walls of our communities. Our partnerships in professional organizations expanded the lenses from which we view the world.

These partnerships with professional associations and organizations have allowed us, and allow leaders in general, to unlearn formerly myopic views of the world. Our connections and unlearning the old leadership style has allowed us to embrace multiple viewpoints in all that we do.

Whether in attendance at a White House Makerspace event, or in a community meeting at the local senior center, our experiences have guided us in new and powerful ways. These partnerships open doors, create pathways for improvement, and set the stage for multiple connections. Through #supt-chat, the IASA, the AASA, and other partnerships many leaders have been able to unlearn and relearn with each other's support.

A powerful byproduct of these partnerships has included exposure to incredible people and leaders that disconnected leaders might never experience. These partnerships allow leaders to learn from innovative cutting edge thinkers and doers at Google, the EdTech Team, the executives at the IASA, AASA, leaders at Harvard, MIT, Apple, Discovery Education, the White House Office of Policy, Science & Technology, authors, and thoughts leaders too numerous to list.

From one of these experiences, Mike is quoted:

"It was more than telling a leadership story and more than an elevator speech," Lubelfeld said. "I appreciated hearing a real candid review from other superintendents, and Yong Zhao and Heidi Hayes Jacobs. "To me, it was a meaningful exercise. It was a critical conversation and a great practitioner challenge." Part of AASA's mission is to help superintendents excel on the job and help their school districts get to the next level. According to Lubelfeld, he received "next-level leadership expertise."

Retrieved from: http://www.aasa.org/headlinecontent.aspx?id=37802.

The unlearning leader goes to where the smart people are to get better and to learn new ways to lead. The unlearning leader accepts vulnerability as a strength not a weakness. The unlearning leader seeks out and appreciates the power of groups and associations whose mission is to support their members. We are so grateful, humbled, flattered, and appreciative of the myriad experiences afforded us through these partnerships and association leaders.

Nick's team at Leyden is supporting a foundation for the new economy. As featured at a July 2016 Digital Consortium gathering, he showed the group of distinguished leaders both a student-run tech support program and an advanced metals/manufacturing lab where technology and education come together:

> The group visited West Leyden High School on the first day of the meeting to learn about the district's Tech Support Internship (TSI). Students who enroll in TSI acquire hands-on technology experience, and provide tech support to teachers and students. On the same day, attendees visited the metal lab, which prepares future engineers by building their expertise through machinery.

Retrieved from: http://aasa.org/LeadPrograms.aspx?blogmonth=8&blogday=1&blogyear=2016&blogid=84012.

Other powerful byproducts of these partnerships are the sharing and learning of best practices. Whether it's how to begin a 1:1 program or how to increase student agency in decision-making, these unlearning leaders have friends, colleagues, confidants all over the nation with whom they can call, vox, tweet, text, hang out, etc. at a moment's notice. Unlearning leaders are leading tomorrow's schools today through new practices in support of our future.

TEACHING AND LEARNING CONFERENCES

We are often reminded of the "need for training" as an expectation or a barrier to implementation and acceptance of new, innovative educational and instructional opportunities. What sets technology apart from traditional instructional applications, is that in most cases, the technology simply needs to be used. There is not a "sit and get" type of training that is going to yield the type of usage that today's students need, demand, and understand.

Training in and of itself is not a bad thing. Training is not unnecessary, but one's notion of training from an old school model does not fit anymore. Today's model of training looks more like a design that Lev Vygotsky and other constructivist theorists would describe. They would proffer that in order to learn, one must do, scaffold, share, discover, and do again. These theorists support the notion that learning is sustained when the learners are creating their own knowledge.

Think about the instruction manual for the iPhone, oh wait, there isn't one! The world has changed and it is incumbent for leaders to change too. The concept of differentiated instruction as applied to professional learning has made huge positive impacts in the systems where we serve. The concept of a menu approach to professional learning has yielded new and impactful structures around institute days. The teaching and learning conference approach is modern and impactful.

As mentioned, in Deerfield, their team recommended a revamping of the district's professional learning structures. With input from focus groups of teachers coupled with survey data and also with knowledge of best practices through connected leadership, the district embarked on an improvement journey that included the Deerfield College, Deerfield University, and the teaching and learning conference approach to inservices and institute days.

The teaching and learning conference was successful for many reasons: teacher voice drove the structure, teachers were the instructors, leveled or differentiated sessions were available, and professional partners were included. Teachers had a menu of workshop sessions from which they could choose to attend and learn. Unlearn control, let the adults and the students have voice and choice, and watch the results.

The teaching and learning model has been so well-received that the majority of sessions are recipient driven. The majority of experts are our own staff members! The reality that there is expertise in house and that there are experts all around us is a reality that needs to be relearned. In addition, the concept of workshops and classes at varying levels reinforces the value of learning at all levels.

SUMMARY

As a recap, in this chapter we share how the unlearning leader makes an unlearning organization better by listening, changing structures, and personalizing learning opportunities for all. The one day, shot in the arm workshop does not do anything except cost a lot of money. Only through sustained, meaningful, job-embedded professional learning experiences can true innovation, transformation, and change take place.

In chapter 6, we are focusing on unlearning leadership itself as pulling together the main learning elements of the entire book. Ideally you are now more energized to do leadership differently and support a new mindset supporting unlearning. Perhaps you are using the beginning of chapter reflection questions with your leadership team. Regardless of when you start reading the book we hope you will stop by #suptchat on the first Wednesday of each month to engage with a broader PLN.

S—Stop and reflect on the central ideas of this chapter and think about how you will implement one or more of the suggestions. Ask yourself:

- What could your staff teach other during an institute?
- What professional organizations should you connect with on a deeper level?
- Have you looked at badging or microcredentialing in your district?

U—Understand the importance of seeking out what is working in other districts and going to visit them. Understand that you can learn what to do, and sometimes more importantly, what not to do when you meet with districts that have already done what you are trying to do.

P—Plan to get more involved in your state and national professional organizations. When you get involved, your PLN grows, and you become a better leader at home.

T—Think of a key take-away from this chapter. What will you bring back to your team for discussion?

Chat: Pick an edchat, like #ditchbook that meets Thursdays from 10:00 pm to 11:00 pm CDT. This is a chat where educators discuss ways to use digital tools and other open educational resources to ditch traditional textbooks.

PRACTITIONER COMMENTARY—KRISTINE GILMORE

Dr. Kristine Gilmore is the superintendent of the 5,800 student DC Everest Area School District in Weston, Wisconsin.

In 2002 when I began as Superintendent at DC Everest, we provided teachers with general professional development opportunities. This included one-time speakers, a few selected individuals attending conferences, trainings around textbook adoptions, and a monthly early release schedule. Actually, we really didn't think a lot about our teachers as learners. They were the experts, and we mostly "hoped" they would figure things out.

Somewhere along the way, we finally saw the light and decided to really **invest** in our teachers. We know our teachers make the biggest difference in our students' lives. We decided we can't and won't leave things to chance. Our teachers are adult learners and also need the same things our students do: a sense of purpose and meaning, ownership, individualization, and learning personalized.

How do you do this in times of accountability, reform, and limited resources? I believe it is by taking full advantage of your current situation, prioritizing resources, seeing the good in people and just moving forward. If it is good for kids and your employees—make it happen!

In 2011, the Wisconsin Legislature drastically changed and reduced collective bargaining rights for public school employees through ACT 10. This situation was perceived as mostly negative for school employees; however, it did provide the opportunity for districts to rebuild archaic salary schedules.

We could have sat around feeling sorry for ourselves—but we found the silver lining. Since that time, we listened to what teachers wanted and a collaborative team built a compensation model around individualized professional development. This compensation model is based upon each teacher's own plan of development with the support of the individual's supervisor.

So, what does that mean? Teachers accumulate professional development hours (outside of the school day) by attending in person and online professional development seminars, mini courses, degree programs, teaching and learning conferences, creating supervisor approved action research, visiting schools, teaching other teachers, and participating in Vanguard and Digital Leader Corps groups.

Teachers select professional development around their individual goals and the needs of their learners. Movement on the compensation model is based on 90 hours of professional development. Last year 410 DC Everest teachers voluntarily participated in 25,700+ hours of professional development outside of the school day. I was overwhelmed by the interest, commitment, and sheer desire to learn from our teachers.

Anytime you drove past the PD Center the parking lot was full of cars, including nights and weekends. When I asked teachers how they felt about the compensation model a common response was "I feel like the district supports me in becoming a better teacher" and "I feel invested in as an employee."

A few things come to mind when I think about how we made this happen and how we will continue to improve in the future.

1. Our school board, administration, and every employee support the learning of others. The board made the commitment to purchase a professional development center for our staff and committed to the finances to provide the professional development and compensation model. We send the message to our staff that we are investing in you.
2. Time is one of the greatest resources we can give our teachers. All teachers need time to participate in professional learning communities.
3. We value the expertise of our people. Teachers and administrators who would like to provide professional development are offered a stipend or double professional development hours. There is nothing more powerful than learning from each other and watching people support one another in the classroom.

4. We cannot do this alone. We have created strong business partnerships with valuable companies like Discovery Education and Apple who are committed to the success of our district. They provide invaluable learning experiences and expertise in the areas of pedagogy and digital transformation. As things continue to change so quickly, we will need to rely more on outside partners.

5. Relationships, relationships, relationships. We need each other to do this work. We have built strong relationships with professional associations, local colleges, and other school districts to provide resources. This past year we sponsored Let's Go Wisconsin, a multi-day conference for thirty Wisconsin districts who are 1:1 with Apple products. We are stronger by sharing our expertise. Districts need to support one another and share resources.

6. Learning takes place in many ways. Some people enjoy traditional courses and others participate in twitter chats, online forums, and independent study. We are providing our staff the same options we want for our students.

7. Visiting other schools and being visited can be a powerful tool. It is always exciting to hear the chatter after a site visit to another district and to see the wheels in motion. It is also empowering to see the pride and recognition of great teachers sharing their best practices with others.

8. Take risks, fail, and try to be better. We need to model that things seldom go perfectly, but how we respond is the key to resiliency and continuous improvement.

9. Learn from your colleagues. Beg, borrow, and steal the best ideas. Create a network of positive leaders and surround yourself. This can be done through state and national professional organizations. Go virtual: get on Twitter, Voxer, or whatever medium connects you.

This journey has been extremely exciting for our district. I truly believe all employees want the opportunity to grow in their current position and it is the responsibility of the leadership team to make sure these opportunities exist. Ask your employees what they need—they will tell you and then GO MAKE IT HAPPEN.

As an *unlearning leader*, be courageous and give yourself the permission to blaze new trails.

Chapter Six

Unlearning Leadership

When he took time to help the man up the mountain, he scaled it himself.

—Tibetan Proverb

Reflection Questions

Are you leading in a culture of openness or fear? Joy or misery? How do you know?

In what ways are you deliberately leading with your core values at the front?

Are you a leader of yesterday, today, or tomorrow?

In what ways does your audience engage with your messages? How do you know?

Stop-Think-Act

Do you have a leadership coach or accountability partner?

Who gives you feedback, honest feedback, about your leadership impact?

If the answers to the two questions above is "I don't know," now might be the time to reach out for a 360° assessment.

THE WIZARD OF OZ

People desire strong leadership. Think of Dorothy, the Tin Man, the Scarecrow, and the Cowardly Lion as they make their way toward the Emerald City in the Wizard of Oz. They have never met nor even seen the wizard, but they believe he is an all-knowing leader who can solve their problems. It turns out that this grand image of the wizard is a sham. He doesn't have all of the answers. He is a stereotypical myth of the high and mighty leader with referent authority.

However, at the end of the story, he does find a way to help each of those main characters. The mentality of a school leader as some Wizard of Oz who lives in the Emerald City (district office or principal's office) with all of the solutions must be unlearned! The Wizard sheds his phony authoritarian power and gets back to the real soul of leadership, relationships, and serving others.

When a school or a school district gets a new leader, everyone in the organization is tempted to feel apprehension. What are her expectations? Will he bring new curriculum or assessment systems? Will she hire some of her friends from her past district? What changes is he going to make to OUR school or OUR district. How will this affect me?

As the new school leader, there can also be apprehension. You might feel like you need to have the plan, the vision, or the answers to all of the problems that exist in the school or community. If we are to unlearn the feeling that we should have all of the answers, what characteristics should leaders have today? If we unlearn the myth of referent power and the myth of the all-knowing wizard, amazing and real change can happen.

FLEXIBILITY

School leaders should have a strong sense of their core values and beliefs. Much of this informs not only the work we do, but also why we do the work that we do. Just as important as knowing yourself, and maybe more important, is the ability to be flexible. That doesn't mean that you ever violate your core values, but it does mean that you are able to become the leader that your school or your district needs you to be.

Let's start at the classroom level. Each teacher has certain beliefs, certain practices, and certain routines. Then thirty students walk in. Not all of those routines and practices will work for every student. In fact, every single student needs something different from that teacher. The best teachers are able to stick to their core beliefs and values while finding ways to be the teacher that each student needs them to be. That teacher is able to identify the strengths and areas of growth for each child and then work to enrich and support them in the best ways possible.

As a building principal, the same value of flexibility applies. Principals need to think about the individual needs of each student as well as the individual needs of every teacher, every parent, as well as a multitude of other employees and stakeholders in the building. The principal might want to allocate her time in a certain way, but circumstances will dictate the need to do something completely different.

The principal might want to put a focus on math curriculum, but if the stakeholders let him know staff morale is an issue, he might be prudent to start there instead. Just like the teacher needs to be mindful of the needs of each individual student, the principal must recognize that teachers and support staff members have varying needs as well.

The first year teacher, the thirty-year veteran, the one-on-one paraprofessional, and the bus driver each need different things from their principal. Leaders need to be flexible enough to identify those needs and be who the others need them to be.

As a leader at the superintendent level, the scope widens, but the need for flexibility is the same. Each school board member, each elected official, each principal, each parent, each staff member, and each student needs something different from you. Your job is to identify and understand those needs so that you can be the best possible leader for all of those stakeholders. You also need to recognize that many of their needs may conflict with one another and you will have to communicate about why you make certain decisions as opposed to others.

When you are the new leader in an organization, it is much easier for YOU to change to be the leader they need you to be than it is for you to change the organization to fit your leadership. Put more simply, you need to become the leader your school or district needs you to be. Those needs will also change from year to year and you need to possess the flexibility to always be the leader that is necessary.

All of this talk about flexibility comes with one huge warning. A leader should never violate their core beliefs or personal ethics. As our friend Dr. Michael Hinojosa, Dallas superintendent and amazing leader, says, you need to know what issues will force you to put your keys on the table and walk away. If your school board or community is asking you to be a leader that conflicts with your beliefs, you need to recognize it as a bad fit and be willing to move on.

VISIBILITY

Let's go back to the Wizard of Oz for a moment. As the leader of the Emerald City, the wizard hid behind a curtain and led from a place of mystery and power. Too many school leaders get caught in the trap of leading behind a curtain in the form of an office door, an off-site district office building, or excuses of why we are too busy. We need to unlearn these excuses and embrace the need to be visible in our buildings. We also support visibility through social media.

An idea that gets the leaders out from behind the curtain in Deerfield is called "Our presence is your present." Annually, after Thanksgiving and before winter break, the leadership team administrators are "raffled off" in each school. Teachers, support staff, or anyone interested can put their names on a slip of paper into a bag with the name of an administrator.

The administrators then gift a full day of substitute work for the employees whose names are selected. The employees may use the day off as a gift. They can use it for personal or professional reasons; it's up to them. Over the past three years Mike has served as a substitute seventh-grade math teacher, as a substitute self-contained special education teacher for grades 3–5, and as a first grade teacher.

The seventh-grade math teaching experience was documented in a Discovery Education blog post:

> *Recently I had the chance to teach students at one middle school in Alan B. Shepard Middle School. I was a 7th grade math teacher that day, and it was awesome. Last year and this year (and next year too) we in the leadership team "raffle" ourselves off to the teachers as a holiday gift and an acknowledgement of their high value. Another rationale/reason for us to do this is based upon our values and beliefs of the importance for us to get back into the classroom and experience a real day in the present time with real students "today" as opposed to looking through the lenses of teachers from a time in the past when we were full time classroom teachers (for me that would be back in 1993-1997).*
>
> *Our motto is Engage, Inspire, Empower – this experience today was all three and more!*

Retrieved from: http://blog.discoveryeducation.com/blog/2015/05/18/back-in-the-classroom-instruction-with-digital-resources/.

Many school leaders are embracing the idea of #shadowastudent. These leaders are "pushing the pause button" in their busy lives and spending a full day with a student in order to see and feel the school experience. By developing empathy for the good and bad aspects of school, leaders can deliberately use their visibility to make improvements in their districts. Karen Ritter is an assistant principal at East Leyden High School. In 2016, she was featured on the PBS NewsHour after spending a day shadowing a student in her building.

Karen learned how it felt to participate in physical education, to eat in the student cafeteria, to move through the building during passing periods, and to take a full day of classes. In her reflections, she noted many things that she learned during the day. Perhaps just as important as her take-aways was the fact that she modeled the willingness to be a visible school leader who is engaged in her school community.

COMPASSION

Being an educator is more than a job, it is a lifestyle, and many believe it is a calling. You never get to stop being a teacher, a principal, or a superintendent. This is true when you are at home, at the grocery store, at a local restaurant, or really anywhere. For some leaders, this reality can feel smothering. We need to unlearn any thoughts of this as a negative and accept our need to be compassionate leaders for our schools and communities.

When Nick was the superintendent for Illinois Valley Central Unit School District in Illinois, he had two impactful encounters regarding breakfast. The pre-school teachers were conducting home visits and they spent some time with a family in a less affluent part of the community. They came back and told Nick how a mother was providing a small can of mandarin oranges as breakfast for her four small children. That "meal" was not enough for one child, let alone all four of them.

Several days later, Nick was in the high school cafeteria in the morning. A new student walked up and asked where breakfast was being served. Nick let him know that the district didn't provide breakfast, but offered to go and get a granola bar from his office on the other side of the building. He expected the young man to say "No, thanks," but instead he said "Yes, please." Nick retrieved the granola and brought it to the student.

At that point, Nick allowed the understanding of those situations to take the form of feeling compassion for the needs of the community. The district had never provided a breakfast program and it was not mandated based on the percentages of low-income students in the district. However, a compassionate leader is able to look beyond the existing realities to do what is necessary. Starting the next year, a breakfast program was implemented and available for the students in the district.

A compassionate leader is one who succeeds when their students and teachers succeed, fails when they fail, cries when they cry, and celebrates when they celebrate. At the end of the Wizard of Oz, the wizard does everything he can to help Dorothy get back home. As school leaders, we need to be compassionate and look beyond our own needs to meet the needs of those we serve.

RELATIONSHIPS

The leader who is able to create conditions for change has built a foundation of trust. Trust leads to relationships. Relationships and relationship building relate to the fifth exemplary practice of leadership from Kouzes and Posner. Encouraging the Heart, the second E in MICEE, is the final of their five exemplary practices.

Leaders are effective when they listen to people and people listen to them. Many writers and researchers have written a lot about leadership. Many studies attempt to scientifically identify what leadership is and what traits, behaviors, and responsibilities are "research-based" with proven effects and impacts.

Research on leadership essentially indicates that the most important attributes of leadership involve relationships. Listening to others, involving others, and building capacity in others based upon their interests and skills are all essential for a leader to be successful. Building professional relationships is foundational for all leaders who hope to find success in education, or any industry where people are involved.

The best advice we could give to an aspiring leader is to listen to the people involved, build relationships with those around you, show respect to all, and value the honor, dignity, and worth of all individuals.

As part of our personal philosophies of leadership, relationships, and relationship building are cornerstones of any successful leadership experience. To that end, our work in all settings has been framed by listening, learning, unlearning, relearning, meeting, understanding, examining, observing, reviewing, interacting, visiting.

Transition and change are challenging concepts for many. Leadership is not easy, but leadership is rewarding. Leadership is not making everyone happy, but leadership is staying focused and building successful relationships. Our impact is the result of the collective work of our Boards of Education and the leadership teams with whom we work. Any success we enjoy should be framed in relation to the support we receive as well as the courageous teachers and support staff with whom we work.

As we reflect on being administrators and public servants, we find the same connections between successful people and relationships. As social beings, we seek the benefits of friendship, mentorship, and collegiality at work, as well as personally in civic clubs, sports, hobbies, and more. The people are who and what matter insofar as leadership and change, and growth and progress are concerned.

On a personal level, we have the good fortune to have served in eight school districts combined over the past 40 years. Each change has allowed us to channel the excitement and possibility about the new beginnings we were about to encounter. What is most exciting about leadership transition and change is that it allows for contributing to another community that has a rich history, strong continuity, and strong community ties. It is always an honor to be selected to join a school district and the wonderful and talented people there.

Our hope has always been to start to build relationships with the people and then find out their needs and wants. Our hope has also been to be able to work together and lead in as collaborative manner as practical in the best interests of the students, faculty and staff, parents, members of the board, and the community in general. Each new opportunity has provided a series of true leadership experiences and opportunities for learning and growth.

In our experiences, and in our practices, we regularly use technology to aid our listening and relationship building. Leading in a culture of connectivity and unlearning old paradigms is all about building relationships through devoting time and meeting people on their own communication platforms. The unlearning leader seeks continuous feedback. An effective example is using surveys or focus groups with stakeholders what they need and want. The needs of the people and their capacity for change comes through in these surveys and engagement strategies.

When we do employee survey work, recognition is often the most neglected dimension by managers. For recognition to be appreciated, it must be timely and perceived as an earnest expression from a caring colleague. Get to know your co-workers as people and understand how they prefer to be acknowledged, recognized, and rewarded. Then catch them doing things right and provide praise with enthusiasm.

LEADERSHIP LESSONS

Great schools need great leaders. In order for every student to succeed, school leaders must unlearn the old ways to learn and practice leadership through innovative methods and courageous actions. What once supported change no longer works. What once made sense no longer makes sense. What once sustained economic excellence no longer functions. "In Anglo-Saxon and Norse cultures, a leader established a reputation in large part by the quality of gifts to his followers and visitors" (DePree, 1992, 140).

The national focus on leadership and connected educators is helping more leaders find their voice and it is allowing greater numbers of leadership success stories. Our school districts have been engaged in the connected educator world and that work has received acclaim through regional, state, and national presentations, awards including: Bammy Nominations, Superintendent of the Year nomination, Superintendent of Distinction, Advanced Placement District of the Year, Chicago Tribune Top 100 Workplaces, National School Board Association Magna Award, Center for Digital Education: Digital Content and Curriculum Award, and more.

We promulgate student agency through impactful and sustained leadership and, in our organizations, we have helped our boards unlearn the old five-year strategic plan model and share lessons for sustained future leadership. We have become national connectors of leaders through leadership fellowships, certification programs, and an international Twitter chat. The Twitter chat for superintendents (#suptchat) serves as a monthly workshop connecting leaders from around the United States and the world highlighting the power of the twenty-first century, modern superintendent's personal learning network or PLN.

The unlearning leader surveys, asks, seeks, listens, reviews, shares, communicates, and leads. The unlearning leader measures student engagement, organizational culture, student academic performance, student emotional needs, student academic growth, teacher performance, administrator performance, board performance, community perceptions, and more. The unlearning leader measures, shares, sets goals and action plans, and measures again.

Leading lessons show us that often simply asking someone for their opinion and then listening to their opinion means the world to the one who is asked. Even when leaders must choose a different path from the input, as long as they authentically listen and consider the input, they are applying collaborative practices. DePree (1992) suggests some gifts leaders can give, including: space, opportunity, challenge, clarity, authenticity, meaning, accountability, and conscience (141).

The unlearning leader is not going to make everyone happy. She/he should respect everyone and truly seek their voice and input. Like the reference to Henry Ford in chapter 3 about input he might have received about a faster horse, he took the input and then unlearned transportation. He led and innovated. He mass produced automobiles and we still refer to "horse power." If Ford had tried to make everyone happy, we might still be riding horses instead of enjoying our current cars and looking forward to driverless vehicles.

A BRIEF LOOK AT GOING 1:1

Much has been written about districts and schools "going 1:1," issuing tablets, computers, or other electronic devices to every student. As the quantity of devices in the hands of students grows, these changes cannot succeed without leaders supporting transformative change for student learning experiences. The focus needs to be on content first, and technology second. It is far more important to enhance learning via high quality content and instructional transformation than to simply replace a pencil and paper with a tablet and hope for the best.

There have been many blog posts in the wake of #pencilchat on Twitter, where educators and others discussed the popular "pencil analogy" regarding technology in the classroom. The points made (no pun intended) in this discussion are varied, but an important theme emerged: simply putting pencils in children's hands won't make them great writers.

However, if you give a student a pencil coupled with powerful, meaningful content, and exceptional instruction from an energized and committed educator, a great writer may just emerge. When that occurs, is it the pencil or the instructional content that deserves the credit?

Through site visits and connections with others implementing change and best practices we can all unlearn what we think is right and reimagine education. For example, on a site visit to a local school system, teams from Deerfield learned what a classroom can look like. They unlearned a non 1:1 setting through observation and interaction. An example was shown in a fourth grade classroom where the students were interacting with "The Gallon Man," a construct meant to help students learn about the liquid measurement system.

The students were working in cooperative groups with one computer per group. They had the teacher's instructions on a video so they could listen to them as many times as they wanted. The students were also cutting with scissors and construction paper, pasting and gluing, and creating their own Gallon Man. The lesson was engaging and all of the students were working on listening, speaking, cooperating, creating, etc. Technology was a tool in that lesson, but learning was the focus.

As Andrew Marcinek writes in his book, *The 1:1 Roadmap: Setting the Course for Innovation in Education*:

> Technology is more than just "Computer Class"; it is a literacy that must be threaded throughout the fabric of a school. In a 1:1 environment, you're preparing students to be responsible citizens of the physical and digital worlds. But it's easy to get overwhelmed with devices; you have to have a plan for technology that keeps learning at center stage.

Marcinek's point regarding keeping the focus on learning cannot be lost in the rush to embrace EdTech as a panacea. Though we are strong advocates for instructional change as the catalyst for a substantive change in student outcomes, content is as important as instruction in the classroom. Content is curriculum, content is resources that support curriculum, content is what is being taught in our classrooms.

The unlearning leader ought to follow case study examples from across the country where districts are successfully impacting and affecting meaningful innovation and change in the 1:1 environment, as well as in general.

SUMMARY

As a recap, we have traveled the yellow brick road for nearly five decades in traditional settings. The five exemplary leadership practices as presented in Kouzes and Posner's *Leadership Challenge: Model the Way, Inspire a Shared Vision, Challenge the Process, Enable others to Act, and Encourage the Heart* permeate our learning, unlearning, and relearning as leaders.

The lessons found in these chapters are meant to highlight and emphasize the facts that change "inside the box" can be done! Change as a process must be understood, discussed, and addressed at each step through direct and clear communication. We submit that the unlearning leader is leading for tomorrow's schools today! In the conclusion that follows we recap the main ideas and lessons from the book as well as share a call to action. We hope you will unlearn with pride, passion, and power.

S—Stop and reflect on the central ideas of this chapter and think about how you will implement one or more of the suggestions. Ask yourself:

- Do I know what it feels like to be a student or teacher in my district?
- How do I make sure to be present in my buildings and classrooms?
- Am I able to compassionately share in the successes and challenges of everyone in my district?

U—Understand that leadership is different today. We cannot expect other people to change to meet our leadership style. Instead, we need to identify what people need from us and we need to adjust to be the leader they need us to be.

P—Plan to spend time with the people in your district. People need one-on-one access with you as well as seeing you at events, in the hallways, and in the classrooms.

T—Think about who you want to be as a leader. What practices do you need to unlearn and what characteristics of great leaders do you want to emulate?

Chat: Pick an edchat, like #iledchat which takes place every Monday night with educators from across Illinois. Many similar chats exist for other states as well. For ease in chatting via Twitter, use Tweetdeck. A reference guide is located in Appendix A.

PRACTITIONER COMMENTARY—MATT MAYER

Dr. Matt Mayer is the principal of the 500 student Kenneth Murphy Elementary School in Beach Park, Illinois.

Educational leadership. This is a phrase often found in many educational institutions' course guides. Unfortunately, the two words have not been synonymous until recently. These institutions structure programs to allow leadership students to learn about past practices of highly effective educational leaders.

Contrary to this, much of the literature used within these courses is focused on leadership but little translated to more than managerial tasks to be completed. The successes of leaders highlighted in these courses were rooted in times when critical-thinking, collaboration, communication, and creativity were not necessary skill sets that needed to be developed and nurtured within children.

Educational leadership within the twentieth century was almost entirely centered upon being a strong manager within the organization. New leaders often enter the profession believing that these approaches are the most effective at leading an institution. To compound this further many within the profession still continue to exist as twentieth-century leaders or as I call them managers.

These leaders often find comfort from leading from their office and engage in processes and procedures that seek to advance their individualized ideas. This group has led to stagnation and learning and consistently avoids any effort of embracing innovation and exploration. This group is quickly becoming and should be extinct.

Educational leadership is not about managing any longer. So often leaders feel as though they need to be the person wearing the cape that is going to deliver the school to new positive and unknown horizons. This belief that there is a superhero leader that is able to transform schools single-handedly is categorically incorrect.

For schools to truly become highly effective, leaders need to work to distribute leadership and build the capacity of the teams they surround themselves with. Twenty-first-century leaders need to reflect upon their strengths and weaknesses and have the humility to find those individuals that will complement their abilities while also moving the organization forward.

To truly lead within an institution, it is imperative for those individuals to be great at following. It is imperative that these leaders are able to adopt steps to empower staff as they work toward innovating in developing practices that are going to move students forward. Twenty-first-century school leadership is going to be the best remembered for collaborative relationships that leaders are able to form and their ability to lead while following the trail blazers on each of their teams.

In addition to not only being willing to lead by learning from staff, truly innovative leaders are finding ways to learn from the students that they serve. School leaders must always remember the importance that needs to be placed upon forming solid relationships with their closest stakeholders. Students within our classrooms possess the greatest knowledge available for truly enhancing our instructional practices. No longer can we look at school as something that is being done to students.

The entire process of educating this next generation of leaders must be forged in a model that allows for co-learning amongst the students, teachers, and leaders within the institution. By harnessing the power of student voice, truly innovative instructional leaders are consistently providing learning opportunities for students that will prepare them to be successful as they transition out of our classrooms and into our workplaces.

Twenty-first-century leading is going to require leaders to embrace significant shifts in the manner in which leadership must exist. Truly effective leaders will never be able to lead from an office or behind a desk. The new mold of leadership is instead rooted in highly visible leadership that places a premium on building relationships and the capacity of others.

These new leaders are going to need to learn how to lead from the front, middle, and behind. True educational leaders are consistently working to grow and develop themselves and their skills. Twenty-first-century leaders should be modeling the importance of professional connections through the use of social media tools like Twitter and Voxer.

This leadership from the front will inspire staff to take steps to consistently improve, which in turn will increase the capacity of the entire organization. These leaders should also embrace the opportunity to lead from the middle of the institution. Leadership from the middle will allow the leader to listen to and learn from those within the organization and will foster a group of educators that consistently feel empowered.

By standing behind staff and fully supporting new ideas and initiatives, twenty-first-century leaders will consistently be leading from behind those whose success is most crucial. Leaders need to consistently assess what is occurring within their organizations and be willing to get behind organic developments that have been established without their direct influence.

This process of leading will ensure that staff feel empowered and the organization is consistently striving to meet the needs of all students. Educational leadership needs to look profoundly different than it does in many institutions.

Conclusion

The premise of this book is that we all need to unlearn because old conventions stymie meaningful change. In addition, learning is very difficult to unlearn. The "wiring" in our brains is hard to alter. Once we learn what is right, it's often almost impossible to unlearn and accept a new right. As we stated in the beginning of the book, our landscape as leaders is applied to school leadership, classrooms, pedagogy, and educational systems in general.

In order to change course and effectively prepare today's youth for tomorrow, we submit that much of what we have learned in general over the course of our lives, education, and professional careers must be unlearned in order to provide a new tomorrow for our nation's children. It's urgent to reimagine education. It's urgent to pack up the nineteenth century and move it into a museum. It's urgent to unlearn so we can create a modern educational system for our nation's youth.

Through anecdotes, case studies, connections with research and literature, we have laid out concrete examples of leading for tomorrow's schools today. Zhao (2016) writes about the principles of a new paradigm (175). Like Zhao, we are proffering the need for a new paradigm—a paradigm where leaders unlearn what used to work in order to move forward.

Ideally, you as a reader have been able to relate to, consider, and connect with some of the learning purposes of the book:

- Energize people to think, act, and do leadership differently.
- Embody an innovative mindset at all levels that supports unlearning.
- Model and share through experience, observation, and trial and error a new way of leading from within the organization.
- Put forth the power and positive impact and legacy for leadership.

- Unlearn old truths to begin to lead in new ways.
- Leverage connection opportunities like #suptchat to lead and learn for tomorrow.

Through unlearning and leading based upon the foundation of the five exemplary practices of leadership as espoused by Jim Kouzes and Barry Posner, we have experienced true systems growth for and on behalf of students, staff, and community. Our passion for paying it forward is embedded on every page in this book. The passion for service and doing good is what calls us to these leadership roles. Together we have learned to unlearn and establish new realities and new structures.

While the systems and structures in place for decades may have helped us, and you, get to where we are today, like the title of Marshall Goldsmith's book: *What Got You Here Won't Get You There.* We strongly believe that unlearning and relearning have supported our success far more than archaic learning. The concept of unlearning resonates with us each and every day as we strive to innovate and impact legacies of success and excellence.

We have discovered that the unlearning leader needs to unlearn connections, the change and planning processes, the way things have always been done, social media and connection tools, professional learning, and much more. The Committee of Ten did a great job, but their work is long past its utility and meaning. We need to create new versions of the Committee of Ten as Dintersmith and Wagner call for in *Most Likely to Succeed.*

Our aim in contributing to the literature on leadership and systems change was to share so that others in like positions can replicate and create organizations where people are energized to think, act, and do leadership differently. The world has changed and it is incumbent upon leaders to change too. We need to raise our expectations and do it. It's time to unlearn that which may have worked in the past, for our future requires new constructs. Kouzes and Posner state,

> You have to believe that what you do counts. You have to believe that your words can inspire and that your actions can move others. And you have to be able to convince others that the same is true for them. (330)

We have discovered that leaders need to unlearn in support of the future of today's youth. Creating new systems and structures will allow the unlearning leader to lead tomorrow's schools today! Our aim is to share, collaborate, communicate, create, and think critically in support of growth, learning, and success.

We hope that after reading this book you have a greater and clearer understanding of how to lead differently. Let's stop talking about twenty-first-century learners. We are already in the twenty-first century. It's time to unlearn the nineteenth century and start looking toward the twenty-second century.

Our complex society presents many challenges to people as they pass from childhood to adulthood. It is our firm belief that a strong educational foundation will support a person's quest for success and prosperity. Young people are our windows to the future. Working with them has helped us see and consider their views as guideposts in decision-making and planning. We are committed to preparing and to supporting our young citizens and their teachers for their future—and ours.

Another aim of this book is service through communication to the world of leaders. Our "stage" has been and continues to be public education, but leadership is leadership. We hope that these words and messages help and inspire leaders in all facets of life! The call to action is simple: UNLEARN. Your students don't deserve the education their parents received. Your students don't deserve the education you received. Your students deserve an education that will prepare them for the future and the world that is waiting for them.

Unlearn.

Appendix A

WHAT IS A TWITTER CHAT?

A Twitter chat is where a group of Twitter users meet at a predetermined time to discuss a certain topic, using a designated hashtag (#) for each tweet contributed. A host or moderator will pose questions (designated with Q1, Q2 ... etc.) to prompt responses from participants (using A1, A2 ... etc.) and encourage interaction among the group. Chats typically last an hour.

IF YOU ARE NOT YET ON TWITTER, PLEASE SET UP A FREE ACCOUNT

https://twitter.com/
Sign up—enter your full name, email and password. (Please make it a strong password to avoid hackers.)

Click on "Sign Up for Twitter"

Choose your username. (We use our real names or initial and name; some folks use their district names.)

Create My Account

You can select interests and hit *Continue* or just hit *Continue* without selecting interests.
You can "follow the suggested accounts" and continue or follow accounts later.

Figure A.1   Tweetdeck.

Step 4 of 5 is up to you—our advice is "skip this step" so you do not have to upload your contacts. Look near the bottom right of your screen—skip.

Step 5 of 5 is to confirm your identity via email and then set up your profile.

Click on the egg near your name and you can set up your profile. We use our photographs, some people use district logos—it's your choice.

Click on Edit Profile (right side of page) to include biographical information, website (district/blog, etc.) and your location—click on Save Changes and you are good to go!

Tweetdeck is an application that is very helpful for engaging in a chat and keeping up.

Tweetdeck is owned by Twitter and integrates seamlessly with your Twitter account as a login.

References

Brown, J.L., Domenech, D., & Sherman, M. (2016). *Personalizing 21st Century Education.* San Francisco, CA: Jossey-Bass.

Bullis, B., Filippi, J., & Lubelfeld, M. (2016a). I Hear What You're Saying ... And I Respect You. *Journal of Scholarship and Practice*, 13(Summer, 2): 44–54.

Bullis, B., Filippi, J., & Lubelfeld, M. (2016b). Reinventing Science Lab Space and Curriculum. *Principal Leadership,* (September): 52–56.

Casas, J., Whitaker, T., & Zoul, J. (2015). *What Connected Educators Do Differently.* New York, NY: Routledge.

Collins, J. (2001). *Good to Great.* New York, NY: Harper Collins.

Couros, G. (2016). *The Innovator's Mindset.* San Diego, CA: Dave Burgess Consulting, Inc.

DePree, M. (1992). *Leadership Jazz.* New York, NY: Dell.

Dintersmith, T., & Wagner, T. (2015). *Most Likely to Succeed: Preparing our Kids for the Innovation Era.* New York: Scribner.

Goldsmith, M. (2007). *What Got You Here Won't Get You There: How Successful People Become Even More Successful.* New York: Hyperion.

Hattie, J., & Yates, G. (2014). *Visible Learning and the Science of How We Learn.* New York, NY: Routledge.

Himebaugh, G., & Lubelfeld, M. (2016). Inspiring a Shared Vision. *Update,* (Spring, Leadership Issue): 24–29.

Jukes, I., & McCain, T. (2007). Beyond TTWWADI. Reconsidering Education in the Information & Communication Age. The Info Savvy Group. Retrieved from: https://www.nesacenter.org/uploaded/conferences/FLC/2010/spkr_handouts/Levinson/ttwwadi-1.pdf

Kohl, H. (2010). *The New Teacher Book.* Milwaukee, WI: Rethinking Schools.

Kouzes, J., & Posner, B. (1999). *Encourage the Heart: A Leader's Guide to Recognizing and Rewarding Others.* San Francisco, CA: Jossey-Bass.

Kouzes, J.M., & Posner, B.Z. (2012). The Leadership Challenge. (5th ed.). San Francisco, CA: Jossey-Bass.

Marcinek, A. (2015). *The 1:1 Road Map: Setting the Course for Innovation in Education*. Thousand Oaks, CA: Corwin.

Nash, R. (2016). *From Seatwork to Feetwork: Engaging Students in Their Own Learning*. (2nd ed.). Thousand Oaks, CA: Corwin.

Polyak, N. (2016). Expanding Your Learning Network via #SuptChat. *School Administrator*, (September): 9.

Sanfelippo, J., & Sinanis, T. (2016). *Hacking Leadership*. Cleveland, OH: Times 10 Publications.

Scharmer, Otto. (2007). *Theory U: Leading from the Future as It Emerges.* Cambridge, MA: Society for Organizational Learning.

Schmidt, F.L., & Hunter, J. (1998). Validity of Various Assessment Tools from: The Validity and Utility of Selection Methods in Personnel Psychology: Practical and Theoretical Implications of 85 Years of Research Findings. *Psychological Bulletin* 124: 262–274.

Zhao, Y. (2016). *Counting What Counts*. Bloomington, IN: Solution Tree.

http://blog.discoveryeducation.com/mlubelfeld/

https://www.deming.org/theman/theories/pdsacycle

About the Authors

Michael Lubelfeld currently serves as the superintendent of schools in the Deerfield, IL Public Schools (District 109). Mike earned his Doctor of Education in curriculum and instruction from Loyola University of Chicago, where his published dissertation was on *Effective Instruction in Middle School Social Studies*. He is also on the adjunct faculty at National Louis University in the Department of Educational Leadership. Mike has earned an IASA School of Advanced Leadership Fellowship and he has also graduated from the AASA National Superintendent Certification Program. He can be found on Twitter at @mikelubelfeld and he is the co-moderator of #supt-chat—the superintendent educational chat on Twitter. Mike has been married to his wife Stephanie for the past thirteen years and they have two children.

Nick Polyak is the proud superintendent of the award-winning Leyden Community High School District 212. He earned his undergraduate degree from Augustana College in Rock Island, IL, his Masters from Governors State University, and his Ed.D. from Loyola University Chicago. Nick has been a classroom teacher and coach, a building and district level administrator, a School Board member, and a superintendent for the past eight years in both central Illinois and suburban Chicago. Nick has earned an IASA School of Advanced Leadership Fellowship and he also graduated from the AASA National Superintendent Certification Program. He can be found on Twitter at @npolyak and he is the co-moderator of #suptchat—the superintendent educational chat on Twitter. Nick has been married to his wife Kate for the past sixteen years and they have four children.

CPSIA information can be obtained
at www.ICGtesting.com
Printed in the USA
BVOW10s1602070217
475542BV00002B/5/P